SHOW ME A HERO

JEREMY SCOTT

SHOW ME A HERO

THE SIN OF RICHARD BYRD JNR

Biteback Publishing

First published in Great Britain in 2011 by
Biteback Publishing Ltd
Westminster Tower
3 Albert Embankment
London
SE1 7SP
Copyright © Jeremy Scott 2011

Plate section pictures copyright and by kind permission of Annapolis Naval
College; Corbis images; Vogue; Superstock; Boston Public Library; Lesley John
Collection; Canadian National Archive; Lincoln Ellsworth Estate; Hank Walker.
Every reasonable effort has been made to trace copyright holders of material
reproduced in this book, but if any have been inadvertently overlooked the
publishers would be glad to hear from them.

ISBN 978-1-84954-130-5
10 9 8 7 6 5 4 3 2 1
A CIP catalogue record for this book is available from the British Library.

Set in Garamond and Riesling by Namkwan Cho
Cover design by Namkwan Cho
Printed and bound in Great Britain by CPI Group (UK) Ltd, Croydon CR0 4YY

For Ramage, who dependably has rubbished nine out of ten of my ideas but nevertheless provided sound editorial advice over the course of two decades and invariably ended up paying for lunch.

CONTENTS

Show me a hero and I will write you a tragedy.

F. Scott Fitzgerald. *Notebooks*

The bad end unhappily, the good unluckily.
That is what tragedy means.

Tom Stoppard

I.

LEADING MAN

The blizzard that roared down from the Appalachian mountains the day before blew out to sea during the night and by dawn the eastern sky is pink and clear. Now the sun, reflected by the canopy of snow covering the Academy's campus, strikes through the high windows to cast a grid of brilliant light across the floor of the gymnasium, where a handful of Naval cadets are hoisting weights, practising on the vaulting horse, or training on the trapeze and rings which hang on long cords from the roof. Caught in one of these bright dusty beams and framed within it as by a spotlight, a young man stands motionless with face uplifted to the blaze.

Unconsciously theatrical, the stance is very flattering; he could be upon a stage. Graced by health and fitness he can carry off the noble pose, for he is uncommonly handsome, with firm chin and a full head of close-cropped dark hair. It's the sort of profile you might see on a Roman coin – indeed twenty years later it will figure on a national medal. Caught in that ray of sun, his face is tilted to watch the gymnast currently performing on the high rings while he waits his own turn to use them. We can make a guess at the period of this sunlit youth from the way he's dressed in narrow shorts and a close-fitting singlet of a cut not seen today; it elongates the line of the torso, and the erect way he holds himself gives the impression he's taller than he is. Perhaps he's aware of this.

As the gymnast on the rings completes his exercise and drops to land on the mat, our man moves into position and makes ready. The feat he is about to attempt is original, devised by himself. Though he has rehearsed the choreography, he has not till now linked its moves in a single continuous routine as he now intends. Nor has any member of the college team of which he is the captain, although they have tried. By virtue of long hours spent in practice he has become a better gymnast than the rest, and to bring off this manoeuvre means much to him. He is ambitious to excel – in this, at Annapolis, in life.

He crouches and springs to grasp the rings, hanging there for a moment before hingeing his body forward at the waist to swing into the movement. This is an intricate stunt he is essaying. It will start with a full somersault, followed by a second then a third, but – and this is the crucial move – as his feet swing upward in this third revolution *he lets go to alter his grasp upon the rings*, and pose dramatically weightless at the summit of his arc… before rolling forward to land gracefully upon the mat below.

He swings into action… completes the first and second revolution, then swoops up into the third. Momentarily the impetus of his body-mass is upward and in this brief gravity-defying instant he releases the rings to change his grasp. One hand connects… the other blunders against the metal, knocking it aside. His body tilts, the sudden drop wrenches his grip from the ring. He falls off-balance, slanted to the side, hits the mat, crumples and goes down, his face a mask of shock. Those near him hear the *crack* as bones in his foot snap on the impact.

The next glimpse of our hero, Richard Byrd, is four years later beneath stormy skies on an autumn day whose blustery squalls are salted with the briny tide-smells of the estuary and whiff of coal smoke from the passing river traffic. Wearing the double-breasted gold-buttoned uniform of a Naval ensign, he is standing a half-pace behind his ship's captain among a knot of others at the head of the gangway of the presidential steam yacht *Mayflower*, waiting to greet the First Executive as he comes on board.

Although he is the youngest and shortest of the handful of officers clustered on deck, and despite the fact that uniforms impose conformity, there is something about Byrd that draws the eye. He is not overawed by the present situation; the importance of the man about to arrive does not unsettle him. True, it is not every day he gets to meet the President, Woodrow Wilson, but this milieu is part of his natural habitat and has been so since infancy. His older brother is a senator; both his mother and father (a state legislator) come from first families of Virginia. A Byrd founded the town of Richmond, another settled the James River estuary, building a palatial colonial house by a plantation employing over a thousand slaves. Wealth and privilege are familiar to Richard Byrd, he has been raised in the family tradition of leadership and public service. That is his heritage and he is aware that he too is expected to achieve eminence; he expects it of himself. We know from our earlier glance at him that he is ambitious, but in the years that have passed since that sighting the seed of ambition lodged within him has hardened, developed sharp edges and grown obdurate. It is not wholly fanciful to compare it to a tumour – as yet undiagnosed and non-malignant, but exerting a pressure which is always *there*. It is not a desire for wealth, property or possessions which drives him but another yet more consuming motivation. He wants to make a name for himself, familiar to the world. What he craves is nothing less than fame.

When asked what heroes risk their lives for, Achilles answered 'Fame'. And Richard Byrd is to do the same. Nor is his situation in any way unusual – since prehistory, men and women have been drawn to celebrity's alluring glow. Yet Byrd's situation is singular, for at this particular moment in the pre-dawn of mass media with its demand for 'personalities', the nature of fame is about to change. Its value will appreciate as the desire for celebrity morphs from wistful longing into craving… finally to obsession. Fame is on its way to becoming what it is today, arguably the most significant driving force in our society. Up there with love, fear, anger and envy among the dominant emotions is a hunger for celebrity.

But this unworthy craving is something Byrd most certainly would not admit to, even to himself. He is no fool, and already preternaturally aware of image. Yet – aged twenty-two, as he stands on the deck of the *Mayflower* awaiting the President – he has a problem in regard to fame: he lacks an opening. The peacetime Navy provides few opportunities for glory to a junior ensign in its service. This is 1914 and America has not yet become involved in the First World War. Nevertheless Byrd has seen action in Haiti and Santo Domingo. When the US intervened to put down revolution threatening its interests in the Caribbean. He has already proved his courage by saving the lives of two men from drowning. He has shown form in a career which has led to this plum posting on the presidential yacht – although the position is due more to a favour President Wilson owed to Byrd's father, an influential supporter in Virginia. Still, it is a prestigious job our man is filling, and appropriately he has just married a woman with a Southern pedigree matching his own, whose political connections will be an asset to his career. Observing Byrd today on the *Mayflower* you would conclude that for someone who wants to become famous in an action adventure role he is in as good a position as any to go for it. Except for one defect…

On the quay below, a stately automobile, followed by another, comes into sight from behind the dockyard buildings to pull up at the gangway. The driver springs out to open the rear door and President Wilson descends carefully onto the cobbled pier. A spare dignified figure in cutaway coat and top hat, he waits for two others similarly dressed to emerge from the vehicle, then moves to the gangway. The President's stern Puritan face remains expressionless as he mounts it slowly, steadying himself with a hand on the rail.

Aboard the ship sounds the shrill whistle of the bosun's pipe. The officers at the gang head snap to attention, the Captain comes to the salute. The President lifts his hat in acknowledgement as he steps on board… then follow handshakes accompanied by a slight inclination of the waist, goodwill all round with instinctive deference, a word or two, and now it is Ensign Byrd's assigned duty to guide the presidential party to their quarters… where in the privacy of his cabin the great man will unbend sufficiently to favour Byrd with what serves for a smile on that grim visage and ask kindly about his father… but that will be in a few minutes when they are below, just now on deck this is still a public setting. The Captain nods at Byrd, and he starts off ahead to lead them to their cabins. A couple of yards in front of the presidential party he steps across the deck… and we realise with a sense of shock that he is crippled: he walks with a limp. Our hero is flawed.

It was a severe disability. That accident in the gymnasium had dislocated Byrd's ankle and broken two bones in his foot. Then on his first assignment at sea he'd broken it again. An operation in Washington fixed the bones with a metal pin but the fracture did not join properly. He trained himself to walk again through a relentless regimen of exercise, overcoming the pain it caused him, yet the limp remained impossible to disguise. It raised questions about his fitness for duty at sea. He refuted his superiors' doubts through his ability to command and organise his men. But the questions remained.

The limp was slight but it was a grave handicap. If he was unable to pass physically A1 at his yearly medicals it restricted his promotion in the Navy. In the world conflict now threatening to involve the US he would not be permitted to serve aboard a fighting warship. No doubt he could obtain a desk job in Washington, but he could never rise far in it. When his classmates became captains of their own ships he would still remain a lieutenant. And what possibilities for action or glory in such a deskbound occupation? What chance for fame?

In 1916 Byrd retired from the active duty list because of his disability. The Navy was good to him. He was made up in rank and given the job of lieutenant in charge of setting up a Naval militia on Rhode Island. He completed the assignment very capably while attending courses in commerce and economics at Harvard graduate school. He was then given precisely the sort of job he dreaded at the Bureau of Naval Personnel in Washington. There he was due to live with his wife Marie – plus now a son – in a pleasant rented house in Georgetown. He would leave it each morning at the same hour, pass the working day making out forms shuffling servicemen from one posting to another, and return home at four o'clock. Every evening he and Marie would attend a party – Naval, military or political in cast – where the male guests would be careful not to drink excessively and the wives not to put a foot wrong. Life would be sociable, civilised, orderly – and stultifying.

He took the job because what else? But he did everything possible to escape from it. He applied for sea duty and was rejected due to the limp. He lobbied to be assigned to US Naval forces in the Mediterranean – and was refused. Though his marriage was good, this was a dismal time for him. Outwardly his manner remained faultless but within was bleakness and frustration. He lost a stone in weight.

Then came enlightenment. The solution to his impediment was already there, and it lay in the air. He applied to train as a Naval aviation cadet. It meant pulling strings because of his medical category but he had not wasted his time in Washington at those innumerable parties; he had already laid down a network of contacts which would prove invaluable, now and in the future. Leaving his family in Georgetown, Byrd travelled south to report to the Pensacola Naval Air Station in Florida. It was a decisive move, the first step of a series that would lead him upward to the stars. He had elevated his crippled being into another element, he had no need to limp if he could fly.

The Wright brothers had made the first flight thirteen years before, in a machine more like a box kite on bicycle wheels than anything resembling an aeroplane. That flight had covered only 260 metres and lasted less than a minute. The newspapers and public had greeted the event with wonder and applause, it was seen as a marvellous stunt, but that this was an invention to alter the nature of warfare and the shape of the future went largely unrecognised by the Army and Navy chiefs and those in government. And by big business. No powerful backers came knocking on the Wright brothers' door with offers to develop their precarious contraption. As a result aircraft design in the US had advanced remarkably little in the interim.

In Europe the invention had been taken up with greater enthusiasm. France and Britain were already ahead in the infant science of aeronautics. The planes being built at that period were so primitive one marvels such clumsy structures managed to stay aloft at all – which frequently they didn't. To date the flying machine had thrilled spectators at displays, dependably supplied newspapers with a steady stream of disasters, in warfare provided an alternative to balloons for artillery observation, and served to promote alarm among enemy forces – though inflicting negligible damage – by dropping crude bombs which the pilot hurled over-board from his open cockpit. Neither in a civil nor a military context had the aeroplane proved itself any real *use*.

The seaplane in which Byrd learned to fly was built of wood with twin canvas-covered wings. Fitted with a single motor, it had a large pontoon grafted to its underbelly which resembled a flat-bottomed punt. Small floats on the wings kept their tips from dipping into the water as the machine lumbered into the air and while landing. Cruising speed was 80 mph. Instructor and student pilot sat in open cockpits, each equipped with a set of controls operating power, ailerons, and rudder worked by foot pedals. The noise of the engine was deafening, communication accomplished only by shouting down a makeshift tube.

Byrd was quick to master the skill of flying; he was a dexter-ous, highly capable if never an *instinctive* pilot. But he was swift to get to *know* a plane, to understand what it could do together with its particular weaknesses and limitations. After obtaining his pilot's wings, which he did without difficulty, he remained at Pensacola as an instructor and had opportunity to study these limitations more closely.

Take-off and landing were when most accidents took place – almost always due to pilot error – but the greatest problem to flight at this time lay in knowing where you were once you were airborne. In cloud or out of sight of land a pilot was lost. Struggling to operate a sextant in an open cockpit and making the necessary calculations on a pad strapped to his thigh while controlling the unstable aircraft with one hand was a haphazard operation at best. And the magnetic compass on the instrument panel was wildly unreliable, for the needle was affected by the iron mass of the engine only feet away.

Byrd applied himself to the task of simplifying the methods a pilot employed to determine his position at any given moment. He possessed a practical systematic brain which he focused on finding a solution. His duties at the air station, where he was now second-in-command, were relatively undemanding. He handled his share of trainee pilots and assisted in the management of the base, but he could be through with work by late afternoon. Parties at this subtropical outpost were few. He was free to spend the evenings on his project. Occupying a bachelor's room and working at night, in the space of a few months Byrd designed three new flying instruments. One was an adapted slide-rule, simplified by removal of all but the figures required for the specific calculation, and enlarging these markings so they could be read more clearly and swiftly. Another device was a sun compass; the third a bubble sextant which utilised the same principle as a spirit-level to provide an artificial horizon if the real one was obscured. Skilled machinists were at hand on the base and he had them construct prototypes. For an amateur inventor working alone (though there *were* no specialists in this new field) and moreover a man uneducated in higher mathematics, it was a remarkable accomplishment. With these tools a pilot could navigate blind for the first time, but Byrd needed to prove this to the Navy board for his inventions to be taken up.

In 1918, a year which would end with the Armistice, a new giant Curtiss seaplane was under construction in the US. The NC-1 would have twin wings with a span of 126 feet and be powered by four 400 horsepower Liberty engines delivering a top speed of 85 mph. Requiring a crew of five, it was capable of carrying a substantial bomb load – or, alternatively, additional fuel tanks to increase its flying range. It was the first of the series of giant bombers the US would adopt as their main strategic weapon to this day. When Byrd first learned of the NC-1 he dared to dream the dream: *he would fly it over the Atlantic, employing his instruments to make the first America–Europe intercontinental crossing.*

Byrd's heroic fantasy was hugely presumptuous; he'd qualified as a pilot only a year before. Yet during that year he had flown almost every day. Experienced pilots were few, and in the infancy of this new profession he was adept as any. Still, he was only a lieutenant and, due to his medical condition, on the active list only under sufferance. He knew himself this was a brazen ambition, one which could only be achieved by enlisting powerful allies.

Brought up in a family long involved in politics, Byrd knew the value of string-pulling, and he possessed a talent for promotion exactly suited to the times. The expense of this project, and the truly stupendous cost of his later expeditions, would all be met through superlative promotion. His imagination was attuned to the popular mind, he understood what the public wanted; bread did not concern him but he knew about circuses. And he possessed an instinctive skill for another modern art, an art so new it didn't yet have a name but would come to be called 'public relations'.

The former football coach at Yale University, Walter Camp, was a national celebrity at this time. Middle-aged, gung-ho and forceful as a pit bull, he regularly exhorted America to get into shape and kick ass. He'd devised a physical fitness programme taken up by many across the country. He'd been a famous figure for years and had contacts with many influential people. Byrd approached him with a proposition. He argued that it must be an American pilot and aircraft that first flew the Atlantic. America was an also-ran in aviation and needed to restore her prestige. Explaining that he was preparing a scheme to put to the Navy, he invited Camp to join him in the project. In return he'd announce to the press that he and the crew were training for the arduous flight on Camp's fitness programme and dietary regimen.

Camp responded warmly to the idea. Not only did it provide

publicity for the product he was peddling, but it was the sort of macho endeavour that exactly fitted his own public image. But he, like Byrd, realised the magnitude of what they were proposing. It so happened that among the people Camp knew was the famous explorer Admiral Peary, and he suggested to Byrd they bring him on board to strengthen their team. Peary had been a childhood role model to Byrd; in 1909 he'd been the first to reach the North Pole. Now in his mid-sixties and long retired from the Navy, he enjoyed a legendary reputation, somewhat, however, tainted by the claim of his former associate Frederick Cook to have got there the year before him. In the light of Byrd's later questionable adventures around the Pole, it is ironic he should have hit upon Peary as exemplar in the role.

Camp and Peary set up a meeting with the Secretary of the Navy. It must have cost Byrd blood not to attend it himself, but it was wise not to do so. He was already mistrusted by his senior officers; he was known to have political connections and to have pulled strings to secure his posting aboard the presidential yacht. There is nothing that Naval brass dislikes more than to be leaned on by politicians, and to learn that this upstart junior had engineered a personal meeting with the Naval Secretary would have united them in cutting him down to size. So Byrd's proposal was made strictly through the proper channels. He presented it to his commander at Pensacola, who endorsed the plan and passed it on to Washington for consideration.

The US was now involved in the war in Europe and American pilots were flying primitive warplanes in France, but all of these were European models; not a single American plane reached France in time to engage in combat. The Flying Corps – existing only as a subordinate, unrespected arm of the Navy – had accomplished nothing to date, and the first crossing of the Atlantic would furnish it with validity, even distinction. The admirals on the Navy Board were aware of the Naval Secretary's wish that the flight should take place but were concerned about the public reaction if it proved a disaster. Failure would reflect upon the Navy. Aerial navigation was an unproved science, and one in which they had no confidence. The Board ruled that, for an American plane to attempt the crossing to Europe, it would be necessary to station picket ships at fifty-mile intervals along its course to provide route markers – and rescue if necessary.

Byrd was exasperated when he learned of the judgement. The Navy was engaged in a war, and it was clearly out of the question to deploy fifty vessels in line across the Atlantic. He realised the Board was stalling in a manner designed not to antagonise the Secretary, a way of avoiding a decision. But his proposal did produce one unlooked-for reaction. He received orders to leave Pensacola, move at once to Halifax, Nova Scotia, and set up a Naval station and refuelling depot on the north Atlantic seaboard. He did not understand what this signified. Had his covert lobbying become known and his punishment was exile? Alternatively, Nova Scotia was the nearest spot to Europe and the logical start-point for a transatlantic crossing. Whichever the Naval Board's intention, he did as ordered. He requisitioned the materiel and equipment necessary together with two seaplanes, had the lot loaded into railroad boxcars, embraced his wife and entrained with his party for Nova Scotia. Once there, his team had the station constructed and habitable in just three days. Byrd chose good men to work with him, then and later. Mistrusted by his superiors, disliked or resented by many fellow officers, his men were devoted to him. And he to them, it must be added. Never matey with those under his authority, he was always conscious of their welfare. He was a fine leader who commanded affection and respect – and got results.

Very soon the station was operational with both planes flying submarine patrols. It was stocked with gasoline, sufficient not just for their own uses but enough to service several of the huge

Curtiss seaplanes now in existence. Meanwhile Byrd saw to his instruments and made ready to pilot a flight across the Atlantic. And then in November came the Armistice. The war was ended.

Byrd was ordered back to Washington to await reassignment. There the pleasure of homecoming was ruined by news that a first air-crossing of the Atlantic was about to start. On 16 May 1919 three Curtiss flying boats took off from Byrd's station at Halifax, on a course for Europe. NC-1 and NC-3 both developed engine trouble and made forced landings in the sea. The NC-4 reached the Azores, where the plane was delayed for nine days by bad weather. It then completed the second leg of the flight to Lisbon. The transit was not non-stop, yet it *was* the first crossing of the Atlantic ocean by air and it proved the effectiveness and reliability of the new instruments used to navigate the course.

But their inventor Richard Byrd had been elbowed off the flight. It was a bitter, crushing blow.

With the end of the First World War the two fighting services, Army and Navy, settled back into their normal peacetime activity of fighting each other.

Not everyone in high command shared the Navy Board's belief that the aeroplane was a weapon of limited usefulness. General Mitchell of the Army, a colourful personality who had made a name for himself in the war, set out to steal the Flying Corps, bypassing his seniors to go directly to Congress with the proposal of creating a national air force under his own command. In high indignation the Navy Board saw someone trying to make off with their toy and in standard infantile reaction protested that they wanted it themselves.

Byrd had enemies on the Navy Board; he'd got up the nose of more than one of the admirals comprising it, but he had friends in Washington together with a network of contacts he'd kept warm during his exile in the wilderness. Washington was the capital of networking and his brother a member of the Senate, but Byrd already knew his way around. With three other pilot officers and the best legal and political advice he composed a draft bill to lay before Congress. It proposed the formation of a separate Bureau of Aeronautics in the Navy Department. He went the rounds, canvassing for support and backers. His was a known face on the circuit, he had a good service record, the Byrd sun compass and other of his inventions were by now standard equipment on long-distance flights, his case was convincing and he was an excellent salesman. He obtained the endorsement of Franklin D. Roosevelt and Naval Secretary Daniels. His indefatigable lobbying ensured the Bill's passage through Congress, though when it reached the Senate General Mitchell did his best to scupper it. But Byrd had gained powerful supporters and it is testament to his political skills that the Bureau of Aeronautics Bill was passed in the Senate. The despised Flying Corps came of age, and it developed into an entity in its own right with its own command.

Byrd was a member of the Bureau from the start. It was a desk job unfitting for a man whose ambition was to be a national hero, yet his desk was sited in a strategic place from which to promote his own career if the opportunity offered. But now the nature of the game had changed. President Wilson had been voted out of office and replaced by a Republican, Warren Harding. The political and emotional climate of the nation had altered, shifted so radically it had become almost another country. For the first time in history, if not the last, America had lost its nerve and was running scared.

The Armistice had been greeted by an outburst of joy throughout the US. Men and women quit their offices to pour onto the
streets and join spontaneous parades. They whooped, cheered and
embraced one another, high on victory. Eight hundred Barnard
College girls danced in a conga-line through Morningside
Heights and couples behaved disgracefully in public places.
In New York Fifth Avenue was solid with celebrants partying
beneath a fluttering storm of 155 tons of ticker tape.

With peace, censorship was abolished, restrictions on electricity were lifted, Times Square and Broadway blazed bright again.
But with defeat of the foreign enemy another enemy was revealed
existing within America itself: Bolshevism. Imported into the US
by immigrants, Bolshevism found ready support among workers
who had been denied the right to strike during the war. Now
they did. In cities and plants all over the country they laid down
their tools and walked out. Their grievances were legitimate:
hours of work were long, wages low and the cost of living had
almost doubled in the last four years. They had been promised a
better fairer world after the war was won – where was it?

Then in 1919 the Red Scare moved into a curiously modern
phase. In his house in Washington, Attorney General Palmer
had just gone to bed when there was a loud explosion outside
his front door. On investigating, he found dismembered limbs
and a headless male torso in a pool of gore on his doorstep.
When the police came they further discovered torn scraps of a
radical pamphlet. Another bomb, this time in a parcel, blew the
hands off a black servant taking the mail to Senator Hardwick,
an advocate of tight immigration controls.

The following year brought an outrage at the very heart of
New York's financial centre, where at the junction of Broad and
Wall Street the Sub-Treasury Building stood beside the US Assay
office. On the opposite side of the road was the headquarters of
J.P. Morgan, the fount of world capitalism; beside it the Doric

façade of the Exchange itself. On the morning of 16 September, a horse-drawn wagon loaded with barrels came down Wall Street toward the intersection. As it drew level with the house of Morgan it exploded with a giant roar. A huge flash of blue-white flame crashed against the street fronts, bursting the windows as it ballooned into the interior. A wall of smoke and dust billowed down the street in a storm of falling masonry, while from all around came the screaming of the wounded hid in the acrid smoke. The Exchange Building quaked in the blast. Those on the floor – where trading was brisk – felt it tremble beneath their feet, then the high windows shattered and the glass blew down on them in a storm of lethal hail. Among the carnage littered across Wall Street were the remains of a horse and splintered fragments of the dray, but the body of the driver was not recovered.

The effect upon the country resembled that of the twin towers. A security which men and women had taken for granted suddenly was no longer there and the world was another place. Very swiftly the Red Scare developed into one of those bouts of paranoid hysteria which periodically sweep America, from the Salem witch trials through McCarthyism in the 1950s to the present day. The journalist Guy Ernpey suggested that the tools for dealing with the Reds could be 'found in any hardware store'. The wave of intolerance spread to affect anyone perceived to be less than 100 per cent American: Blacks, Jews, Catholics. One of Chicago's bathing beaches on Lake Michigan was tacitly divided into two segregated areas. One hot summer afternoon a black boy who had gone swimming there was sprawled on a floating railroad tie thirty yards from shore. Perhaps asleep, he drifted slowly across the invisible frontier dividing black from white. Some white boys on the beach started to throw stones at him. He was seen to push off from the float and swim a few strokes before going under and disappearing from sight. A group of young black men swarmed onto the white beach to attack the stone-throwers. A general melée ensued in which no one was seriously hurt, but this was not so in the resulting race riots which raged through Chicago for a week. There were beatings, stabbings, shootings; homes and shops were torched, thousands rendered homeless and destitute.

Such then was the emotional climate in America at the time when Richard Byrd was seated in his office at the Bureau of Aeronautics trying to work out his personal destiny. The public mood was troubled by the economic recession still persisting three years after the war, poisoned further by the emergence of the Ku Klux Klan and the constraints of Prohibition. Yet, undeterred by the pessimism surrounding him, Byrd came up with an inspiring plan. He put forward a proposal to pilot an aircraft to Europe on a non-stop, solo, intercontinental flight. He argued that the US was so shamefully behind Britain and France in aeroplane design that American-built planes were regarded as obsolescent. It was inevitable that a European machine with a foreign pilot would soon succeed in a first Atlantic crossing, and the most technically advanced nation in the world was about to be publicly trumped. However the *reason* Byrd gave for attempting the flight was to prove that the navigational instruments he'd invented could be operated in flight by a *solo pilot*. A flyer could follow a precise course over the ocean to his destination without need of a navigator. Ostensibly this was no publicity stunt he was proposing but an all-American technological achievement.

The plane he intended to fly was a standard two-cockpit Curtiss biplane, currently in use by the Navy. It had a range of 1,850 miles, but if the navigator's seat was replaced by an auxiliary fuel tank this distance could be increased by an additional 250 miles. These theoretical range limits were calculated for optimum weather conditions, and this could alter drastically in the course of the long flight. It was an alarmingly slim margin to bank on.

Byrd's proposal was ratified by the Aeronautics Bureau and passed to the Chief of Naval Operations, who approved it. Byrd then took it to the Bureau of Navigation – with whom he was on excellent terms because of his instruments – and obtained its necessary agreement for the flight. With these endorsements he took it to the Secretary of the Navy.

But this was not the individual who had been schmoozed by old Admiral Peary and briefed on Byrd's merits by Walter Camp. Another politician, Edwin Denby, now sat behind the desk in that well-upholstered office, and to him Byrd's project looked to be nothing less than the reckless personal adventure that it was. Moreover one likely to end in ignominy when American pilot, American plane and American instruments crashed into the ocean and sank. These were not the headlines the government was looking for just now.

Byrd's project was denied. Once again his path into a starry future was cut off.

Some men would have been crushed by having their dreams so brusquely erased and surely Byrd was disheartened. Yet many Naval officers would have been more than happy with his situation at the time. He enjoyed a Washington posting which enabled him to live at home with his wife and family, he had an important administrative job, and a salary plus living allowance appropriate for the Capitol. As the services scaled down to a peacetime level others had reason to envy the position he occupied.

The Byrds by now had three sons. His salary, together with Marie's inheritance, allowed them to live a highly civilised life in Washington. As a senator Byrd's brother provided access to the right circles, but family connections on both sides together with the contacts he had built up ensured the couple were invited regularly to those parties where it was propitious to be a guest. The job he was doing in the Bureau was valuable, but though it did not show to anyone except Marie, he was bitterly discontent.

His despondency was at odds with what had become a fast-rising mood in the US. Despite the continuing restraints of Prohibition the spirit in America had by now improved remarkably. President Harding's administration, based on insider dealing, graft and corruption, coincided with a soaring economic recovery. From a smoke-filled room supplied with every known brand of whisky a group of Ohio pals lolling in armchairs with waistcoats unbuttoned ruled over a boom of prosperity such as never before had been seen in history. Everything came together to provide it at this time, but it was the machine that made it possible. 'The Roaring Twenties' was one of the names the period was known by, and louder than the strident frenzy of the era was the roar of the machine. Assembly lines and mass production made goods and luxuries available to all, while demand for them rose exponentially sputted by advertising. In America the sun had dispersed the clouds to shine upon a newly prosperous land where the tills were jingling merrily and the sound at night was jazz.

But Richard Byrd was impervious to the optimism enthusing almost everyone. His own future had been frustrated. He was desperately unhappy in his job; he wanted more, much more, and something very different from this. The Navy had failed him, he needed a *sponsor*. But a sponsor for *what*? It must be big; it must tap into public imagination, capture hearts and minds and open wallets. The drama had still to be chosen but he was prepared in his role. He had the looks to be a celebrity, he had the persona and the will for it, and he had working for him the imagery of flight, the fact that the aeroplane was the ultimate machine, the supreme symbol of the age. The aeroplane represented speed, glamour, risk and the cutting edge of modernity itself. Air races, stunt flying and record-breaking attempts were drawing crowds all over the country. Flight was fashion, women tied their scarves to resemble propellers, aviator caps were a style item, goggles a motoring accessory, even an aeroplane-shaped coffin was available. Skywriting – first used by Lucky Strike – had become a medium in itself. New Yorkers woke one morning to an airy message in puffy white script: *Watch the clouds, Julian is arriving from the sky.* Soon after, Hubert Fauntleroy Julian, the first black man to obtain a pilot's licence, flung himself from a plane to land on 7th Avenue at 140 Street dressed in a scarlet Devil costume. Quite *why* was puzzling, but his image scooped the front page.

Byrd knew that his venture must be as far as possible from that sort of stunt, yet it had to capture public attention in the same way: *it must make headlines.* He determined to be the first man to fly to the North Pole. Today flying over the Pole is so commonplace it does not cause you to look away from the in-flight movie to glance at the void below, but then it represented the ultimate destination, the frozen summit of the world. The two Poles were the most inaccessible spots on earth. A flight to the North and back lay at the extreme edge of aeronautical technology. A historic feat, it was charged with as great a symbolism as, decades later, Man's first landing on the moon. No question, if Byrd succeeded in getting there he would return a hero.

Very soon after hitting upon the idea Byrd realised the need to conceal it from possible sponsors. The motivation would be seen as personal and vainglorious and his objective must be masked behind a different plan. He was characteristically pragmatic in the way he approached the new project. To obtain private backing he needed first of all to improve the strength of his hand; only with good cards could he make a pitch for funds. Among the contacts he'd met through old Admiral Peary was Captain Bartlett, who had commanded Peary's supply ship and subsequently sailed Naval vessels to the Arctic on survey expeditions. To him Byrd outlined his scheme, and did so with a becoming modesty toward the older and more experienced man. He was seeking advice, he explained, tentatively suggesting collaboration in an expedition. They would join forces to sail as far north as possible up the east coast of Canada until the ice halted their progress. From that point they would use the two aircraft they brought with them to fly probes into the two million square miles of unexplored frozen ocean lying to the north-west *in search of unknown lands* to claim for the US, together with all they might contain.

Bartlett had acquired a taste for Arctic explorations from his expeditions with Peary, and the idea of blank on the map and an unknown country waiting to be discovered touches a singular spring in the human heart. He was immediately enthused by Byrd's project. He stood in good odour with the Navy and said he knew where he could get hold of a ship; Byrd showed more confidence than he felt in claiming that he could obtain aircraft from the same service. They began at once to refine their plan. As a team the two were credible. Bartlett's track record combined with Byrd's knowledge of flying in Nova Scotia furnished them with the necessary experience. By approaching the new Naval Secretary – no longer the man who had denied Byrd earlier – they stood a good chance of obtaining a ship and aeroplanes for free. What they didn't have was money.

Edsel Ford's office did not much resemble a place of work but looked more like the smoking room of a gentleman's club – except that there was a strict No Smoking rule throughout the premises. This impression of ease and comfort was rudely shattered when the first-time visitor glanced from the windows, which looked out over the uniform roofs of the River Rouge assembly plant which stretched in parallel lines into the smoke-hazed industrial wilderness of downtown Detroit. The prospect was unmatched in its drabness and ugliness, but it was said that when Edsel's father Henry looked at it he did not see the view but only the garden shed behind the house in Bagley Avenue where he'd built his first 'quadricycle' in 1896.

Edsel, a lean-faced dark-haired man of thirty-two, sat at the big library table where he held his meetings, which was spread with an open map, listening to his visitor Richard Byrd. It was rare for a stranger to penetrate this sanctum but Byrd's letter had caused Edsel to receive him with curiosity and interest – as Byrd had been confident that it would. He'd done his research carefully and prepared his pitch to the known nature of the man and his circumstances. And Edsel's circumstances were blessed. The company started by his father at the turn of the century was now producing more than half of America's motor vehicles and had factories spread across the world. Ford had revolutionised the whole process of manufacture by the invention of the assembly line. In 1913 it had taken fourteen hours to assemble a car, one year later it took ninety-five minutes. By now in 1925 Ford was turning out a car every ten seconds across the globe. One in seven Americans owned a car; in this year alone twenty million new autos were registered in the US, three-quarters of them bought on the instalment plan. There were more cars in New York than all of Europe, and every other car in the world was a Ford. As a result of this demand Ford's resources were larger than those of most *countries*. It owned coal and iron mines, forests, glass-making and steel plants, a railroad, a fleet of cargo ships and an immense rubber plantation in Brazil – all in order to control the supply and transportation of its raw materials; the privately owned corporation governed the entire cycle of manufacture from concept to finished product and had a surplus balance of $700 million ($8 billion in today's money).

Edsel had become president of this stupendous kingdom only

five years earlier, though he did not rule it *absolutely*, for Dad still came in to the plant every day. There were sometimes problems with such proximity. Edsel was industrious and capable, but to be born the son of a self-made millionaire, genius and living legend imposes a particular stress upon the psyche; the junior personality must struggle to make its mark.

Byrd's pitch was well tuned for his potential sponsor, and he opened up to him a vista Edsel would not have stumbled upon himself. He spoke of the vast unknown, that gigantic two million square mile slab of unexplored territory which lay adjacent to North America and capped the globe in white. This frozen void might contain new lands, even an undiscovered continent, and if it did surely this must be claimed for the US. There was a strategic argument for possessing such adjacent territory as well as commercial. Who knew what gold, minerals and energy deposits might lie buried there? And was that enormous area *all* frozen. Or might volcanoes exist that warmed the ocean, permitting exposed soil and vegetation? Was life possible in some places? Could there be animal or even near-human creatures which, cut off from the rest of the world for millenia by endless plains of broken ice, had somehow adapted to the hostility of their environment to survive? The unknown is a bewitching concept, for its possibilities are boundless.

Byrd was a skilful salesman and his project was fitting for the times. Prosperity and optimism oxygenated the air that people breathed, and they enjoyed a higher standard of living than any populace had ever known. They shared a belief that tomorrow would be even better and the future was American. Byrd was a convincing persuader and his manner with Edsel, respectful without being deferential, was well judged. He spoke as man to man, not as a supplicant. Explaining his and Bartlett's plans, he claimed he'd secured a ship for the expedition (which stretched the truth, though Bartlett had identified one) and that he was promised three aircraft by the Navy (which was an outright lie), but he knew how to paint a dream and make it live and the dream he painted held allure for Edsel. The idea of 'new lands' appealed to the spirit of monopolistic acquisition which informed the age. He, like all Americans, had pride in his country, he rejoiced in its can-do ethos; this was a time when patriotism was not a dirty word. Edsel saw honour in Byrd's plans: prestige for the nation, for the Ford Corporation – not least for himself. So what did Byrd want from him, he asked.

Hard cash was the answer. Byrd had the props and cast for the production, what he needed was money to mount the show. He could have asked the whole amount he required from Edsel and probably obtained it. In his later writings he is frank about the reason he did not; it would mean sharing control of the expedition with him. Instead he wanted several patrons, all of them men of wealth and influence who would remain his associates in the future. He knew that in a mission like this there could be only one commander. He obtained a contribution of $15,000 from Edsel Ford and hurried back to New York where, a few days later, he acquired a similar sum from John D. Rockefeller, Jnr.

Byrd was not a man who showed his emotions; he possessed a frequently off-putting aloofness and reserve. On the journey home no doubt he sat quietly in the railcar, dignified and, in appearance, calm. Yet surely he must have been brimming over with anticipation and too excited to read the newspaper he held, for his thoughts were soaring in the Arctic. He had every reason to rejoice for he was on his way to the Pole. But the triumph and certainty he felt did not last for long. Only a few days after getting home he received the news that he was not the only contestant in a flight to the North Pole, for another man was planning to fly there before him. He had a rival.

2.

CUE THE OLD CONTENDER

how me a hero and I will write you a tragedy, was Scott Fitzgerald's claim, which forms the epigraph to this book. I intend to run a true story before you which demonstrates the inevitability of this maxim, and the fatal effects upon that hero and those around him. I wish to *show* you these events rather than merely relate them and, just now, the device that best serves is to present the tale as a stage play we are watching from the stalls.

Later, when the action shifts to the Arctic, involving scenes and locations hard to accommodate on stage, we will be obliged to adopt the movie form to convey it. But, at present, the movie form has a particular disadvantage as a medium for the story. Unlike a play, a film provides no *intervals* during which the audience can gather in the crush bar, where – after struggling to obtain drinks – they can discuss the characters, analyse the drama they are watching and speculate on the future development of the plot. And this tragedy merits analysis. Its dynamics are ambition, chivalry, betrayal, the Devil's compact, the price of fame… and these are the strands of eternal myth.

So, to the play. In Scene One the Hero has been introduced on stage and stated his intent. Now the audience returns to their seats, the house lights go down and the rustle of conversation in the auditorium fades to silence as the curtain rises at the start of Scene Two...

The setting we are looking at is the cabin interior of a passenger liner. The wood panelling on the walls is decorated with Art Deco designs and light fittings, the overall tone is sepia. The living space is rather cramped, it would not do for a couple, and while we are taking in its furnishing and period details we realise a little queasily that it is slowly tilting askew. The scene we're watching is slanting at an angle, for the ship we're aboard is at sea. The only figure in sight is that of a grizzled oldster flat on his back on the floor. He's naked to the waist and below that in grey long johns. Hands clasped behind his head, abruptly he hinges at the waist to sit upright, then lie back. Now he does so again... and again... and again... and again... he's engaged in doing 500 sit-ups without pause on the slow heave of the cabin's floor. He has performed the same ritual each morning of the six-day crossing, then followed it by striding for an hour up and down the deserted length of the promenade deck before permitting himself coffee and a frugal breakfast in the dining room. He is one tough disciplined old man.

The workout takes him seventeen minutes to complete and by its end he's breathing deeply but still evenly, though there's a faint sheen of sweat across his shoulders where the sinews show like cords beneath the leathery skin. Today he does not follow with a hike on the promenade deck; this is the morning of the liner's arrival in New York and 500 squats are enough to set up Roald Amundsen for the hassle he knows awaits him there. Still stripped to the waist, he shaves at the cabin's basin where, as the cut-throat razor slices soap from his cheeks in broad firm strokes, the mirror reveals a seamed face weathered to the colour and texture of ancient wood, with a nose like a falcon's beak jutted above the curled flourish of an imperial moustache.

He is obliged to put on a robe and walk a few paces down the corridor to shower; only six of the ship's staterooms possess bathrooms en suite and his is not one of them. The *Drottningholm* is not the largest, the fastest or most glamorous of the liners plying the transatlantic crossing, but she has charm together with a palm court where an orchestra plays in the afternoons, and a certain elegance. Passengers who sail in her – almost all of them Scandinavian or of Scandinavian origin – tend to stay faithful to the ship. 'Like a mellow old country inn', somebody described her to Amundsen.

However, it was not this but a more pragmatic reason which made him choose the *Drottningholm* for his crossing. Following Congress's Emergency Quota Act, which cut off the unrestricted flow of immigrants into the US, the liner had been refitted to suit the changing times. Steerage class was eliminated together with third and the ship rebranded as a 'Cabin Class Liner'. And therein lies the motive for Amundsen's choice; if he had sailed on the *Mauretania* or the *France* he would have been inexorably obliged to go first class. On the *Drottningholm* he can travel more cheaply without looking cheap on arrival in New York. There will be photographers and reporters at the pier, some may have come to photograph or interview *him*. That is, if Mr Keedick had done any sort of job for the 25 per cent he was getting on this venture to New York.

Amundsen has never met Lee Keedick of Keedick Associates Inc., who have set up his coming lecture tour of twenty-five American cities. Arrangements were made by letter, and in the course of the correspondence Mr Keedick was frank in his appraisal of the tour's success. Amundsen's credentials as a speaker were excellent, the very best, Mr Keedick assured him, and the subject matter of the proposed talks was both thrilling and inspiring – he himself was frankly awed by the scale of Amundsen's accomplishments – but there was... no, not a *problem*, Mr Keedick had been careful to avoid that word, he had described it as 'a reality we've got to take on board', namely the fact that these triumphs had taken place fifteen or more years ago. In the nicest possible way Mr Keedick hinted at an eternal truth: human memory is *short*. And perhaps especially so today in the Roaring Twenties when the movies, jazz, dancing and petting offer numerous on-the-spot alternatives to sitting on a hard chair listening to a guttural Nordic pundit droning on for one and a half hours about the past with not a hope in hell of a drink before or after.

While dressing in his cabin Amundsen feels the vibration of the ship's turbines slow to a pulse as the *Drottningholm* reduces speed on entering the Verrazano Narrows. His suitcases are already packed; he insisted on doing so himself, but when the steward comes to take them he tips him $5 for his services during the crossing. Tugs, lumber barges, sandscows and tramp steamers crowd the water. Seagulls wheel and cry above the shipping. The *Drottningholm*'s siren salutes the Statue of Liberty with a double hoot and the liner slides into relief against the pinnacles and towers of the Manhattan skyline. Its turbines disengage and tugs take control of the ship, shoving it sideways through a slick of splintered crates and rotting vegetables, cans and tide-wrack to butt the vessel alongside Pier 97, with its Customs Shed and quay thronged with a happy crowd to welcome the arriving passengers. Amundsen squares his shoulders, draws in a deep breath of hot polluted air, puts on his bowler hat and marches down the gangway into America. The year is 1924.

This, he plans, will be his last adventure; the final expedition to redeem his career. Judged by any standard it is quite some career already. He was twenty-five and mate of the *Belgica*, the first ship to winter in the Antarctic, when she was trapped in the ice for thirteen months while the entire crew became incapacitated by scurvy and two of them went mad. Thirty-one when, oppressed by debt and hounded by creditors, he'd severed his ship's mooring cable with an axe, slipped out of harbour by night to escape them, and sailed to navigate the North-West Passage around the top of Canada to the Pacific – a voyage men had been attempting, failing, and dying to accomplish for 400 years. But his ambition since adolescence had always been the North Pole. In 1907 he began to set up an expedition to achieve it, borrowing a ship from his mentor Fridtjof Nansen, but his plans were thwarted when in September 1909 he learned that Peary had reached the Pole, claiming it for America. It was a bitter blow, for in that instant Amundsen's projected book and lecture tour about the journey – and with them any hope of paying off his debts – all went for naught. There was no prize for coming second. Instead, Amundsen decided to go south. He told no one except his brother. Not his backers, not the ship's crew, not even Nansen – who later would see it as a betrayal, for he'd nurtured the same dream himself. There was no time for Amundsen to convince them of the rightness of his plan and obtain their agreement; the English explorer Captain Scott had already set out on an expedition with the same aim, to be the first to reach that yet unconquered Pole. Amundsen reached it one month ahead of Scott, winning the prize for Norway, though killing and eating his dogs along the way as they became redundant to pull the sledges with their diminishing loads. His action was pragmatic and necessary but it gained him a bad press afterward, particularly in England where he was branded a callous unsporting foreigner, a rotter. Nevertheless he *was* the first to get there. But Amundsen's triumph was eclipsed by the heroic tale of Scott and his party's death on their return journey from the Pole. When he learned of their stirring end Amundsen's dismayed reaction was, 'He's won!' And he was correct, for it was Scott's story which gripped the heart and became history, not his own.

These events are behind him, that was Amundsen's career. Now is different. His situation today is unendurable to a proud and haughty man. Not only is he ruined and oppressed by debt, but discredited – wrongly – by charges of fraud. His honour, which when all else was gone alone sustained him, brutally has been stripped from him. Only courage remains to him, and tenacity. He is fifty-four and old for the rigours of the ice, but his body is fit and hard and his will implacable as ever it has been. He has one expedition still left in him, one final opportunity to recover his fortune and reputation before going down in the shipwreck of his life. One last shot at vindication, win or lose. One flight of Icarus… to the North Pole. That is Amundsen's plan, to be the first to fly there in one of the primitive aeroplanes or airships of the day. He has come to America to raise the wind.

There *were* news crews waiting on the crowded pier as Amundsen stepped ashore. Two teams, each of assistant and operator in flat caps cranking the bulky camera on its wooden tripod, and there were photographers and the flare and whiff of flash – but they were not here for him.

All around was welcome and emotion of homecoming as he made his way past reunited couples, families and children to the Customs Shed, whose pitched roof lidded in the heat. His own wardrobe did not run to summer clothing, lecturing in this weather would be an ordeal. Other men waiting for their luggage were dressed in seersucker or linen suits. And they wore trilbies or straw boaters, not bowler hats. The women were in light summer dresses with dropped waists, bright with colour. He was unused to colour if not to the sight of women smoking – though Eskimo women squatted puffing pipes of shag, not cigarettes extracted from gold or silver cases and fitted into long holders by manicured fingers with painted nails. In New York City the natives were a species new to him.

His luggage was cleared. A porter wheeled the cases to a line of waiting cabs, the driver strapped them on the roof. 'The Waldorf', Amundsen told him and stepped up into the back. He sat with a straight spine in his tightly buttoned three-piece woollen suit, looking out the open window as they rode cross-town through streets dense with autos, vans, trucks, buses and still a few horse-drawn drays. The air smelt of gasoline and crushed dung. The sidewalks were thronged with people, with clamour and vitality. All were walking with intent. No one *strolled*. Noise was every-where, a deafening roar vibrating on the air, you could *feel* the noise. He travelled through the din and clatter of a city strident with vivid life and voices yelling above the racket. Vendors were selling food from barrows on the sidewalk and the smell of cook-ing and fume of car exhausts lay trapped between the buildings where empty spaces showed like missing teeth – sites busy with concrete mixers, dump trucks, power shovels, pneumatic drills, and swarming with men stripped to the waist. The economy was booming, on almost every block the old was being done away, new buildings going up. As was the stock market, buying shares had become a recreational sport, like betting. Turning into Fifth Avenue the cab was halted in traffic filtering by a huge hole in the road, fenced off by hurdles. The top plank of each explained: DIG WE MUST FOR GROWING NEW YORK.

As the taxi drew up outside the Waldorf Astoria at 34th Street a uniformed doorman strode from the shade of the awning to open its door, while snapping his fingers to summon a bellboy for the luggage. Paying off the cab, Amundsen crossed the side-walk and stepped through the hotel's gilded doors into the muted calm of fully realised opulence. The Waldorf's founder, William Waldorf Astor, was a connoisseur of hotels. He'd frequented the very best, and when he conceived his dream to build the grandest and finest of them all he demolished his own mansion on Fifth Avenue to ensure its location was the most fashionable in Manhattan. And thereby set a trend, for hotels became a plutocrat's must-have, a millionaire's collectible. Engaging in the competitive hobby, William's cousin John Jacob Astor IV bought and demolished the adjoining city block to put up the Astoria, adding 550 bedrooms and 400 baths to the Waldorf's 450 (half of which had private bathrooms) and linking the two hotels by a sepia-lit hundred-yard promenade columned and walled in amber marble, the last word in turn-of-the-century elegance. A climate of money enfolded Amundsen in the lobby, which was fragrant with cigar smoke and the scent of expensive perfume. This was the kingdom of the stylish and well-heeled. As he signed the register a note from Lee Keedick was given him, acknowledging if not exactly welcoming him into the domain, hoping he'd had a good crossing, enclosing a schedule, looking forward to a socko tour… and he'd call in the morning. A bellboy took him up to his room and he was alone in five-star luxury.

Unpacking, he hung up and put away his clothes. He could have done with a drink but his room, and all America, was dry. Just now a drink would be appropriate; New World, new adventure, new goal etc. *But same problem*, same problem as had dogged all his expeditions, every damned one of them. But this time it was worse. He was here to find the money to fly to the North Pole… and he was bankrupt. He didn't have a cent to his name, he was busted wide.

The opulence surrounding him was unfamiliar, an alien environment. He was used to alien environments, he could mould his will and his hard old body to endure anything, he could surmount the perils of the Arctic, but here was different. Planning had been the key to his explorations, meticulous attention to every single detail that could be worked out before the adventure started, and from that had come the habit of trusting no one to pack for him. Preparation was all. He knew nobody in Manhattan well enough to telephone, but to remain in his hotel room was idle and profitless when he could reconnoitre the territory where he had come to score. Taking the elevator down to the lobby he stepped out into the stifling heat of the afternoon and started up Fifth Avenue on foot. An old man in a city that bounced with youth, he was Rip van Wrinkle stumbling from his long sleep into a world that had become unrecognisable. It didn't even *look* like any place he knew.

Something unprecedented had happened at the start of the Twenties, something wondrous and magical which transformed everything. Autos, jazz, movies and radio – mass communication – reinvented America. A generation came into being which was nothing like its parents, neither in the way it looked or how it acted or what it expected out of life. It expected fun. It expected *things*: possessions, music, dancing, opportunities and stylish clothes. And suddenly for the first time in the history of the world all of these were available and to hand. The Fifth Avenue Amundsen walked up that sunny afternoon had been trans-figured in appearance by plate glass. Store windows displayed a dazzling extravagance, within their interiors the fussiness of the Belle Époque had been replaced by the elegant swirls of Art Deco; style had become commodity. This was the glorious dawn of consumer culture and powering it was that other force which impelled the era: advertising. As Woolcott Gibbs wrote in the *New Yorker* (launched early that same decade): 'Advertising was the new giant loudspeaker of American free enterprise, the full-throated blaring horn telling millions what to eat, what to drink, what to wear.'

Amundsen made his way up the sidewalk through a bustle

of pedestrians, straw hats, sunshades, summer dresses, bright colours. People looked different to the way they had before – especially women. They plucked their eyebrows and cropped their hair short as a boy's. The truly fashionable appeared to be without breasts or waist, to have neither thighs, hips nor buttocks. They painted their faces with lipstick and rouge. There were 1,500 brands of face cream and 2,500 perfumes available; a woman bought on average a pound's weight of powder every year. Girls drank cocktails, manhattans, sidecars, martinis and white ladies; before the First World War no one drank anything except sherry before dinner. They necked, petted, put out and thumbed their noses at propriety; according to a magazine survey of the period one in ten carried a contraceptive in her handbag.

Social as well as sexual behaviour altered. Instead of entertaining at home people went to restaurants and night clubs. High society no longer set the tone. Showbiz and gilded youth fused into a new milieu in which 'social position is more a matter of presence than prestige', as Walter Winchell put it. His rival columnist Cholly Knickerbocker, brooding on a barstool in the Ritz at the very start of the decade, named the swanky coterie 'café society' – and the name stuck. Breeding and background were relegated to dullsville, publicity and celebrity became the values of the age.

This was the America to which Amundsen had come; the streets of Manhattan he walked crackled with vitality, optimism and zip. To picture the scene, the cast, and the quick-stepping bustle of the sidewalk as a grind-organ fills the street with music, call to mind the movie *Some Like It Hot*, set in that same era. But it was Scott Fitzgerald who, better than anyone, defined the time and place where the veteran explorer had landed: 'America was going on the greatest, grandest spending spree in history … the whole golden boom was in the air.' The future had become the present, and Amundsen in his tight old-fashioned suit had stepped right into it with nothing in his pocket.

꧁꧂

Six weeks later he was back in Manhattan.

> My depression reached its climax upon my return from the lecture
> tour. The tour was practically a financial failure. My newspaper
> articles had produced but little revenue. As I sat in my room in
> the Waldorf-Astoria, it seemed to me as if the future had closed
> solidly against me, and that my career as an explorer had come
> to an inglorious end. Courage, will power, indomitable faith –
> these qualities had carried me through many dangers and to many
> achievements. Now even their merits seemed of no avail. I was
> nearer to black despair than ever before in my fifty-four years of
> life. As I sat in my room, musing in this way, the telephone rang…

It was the front desk to say that there was a gentleman to see
him, a Mr Lincoln Ellsworth.

The stranger explained himself by saying he'd met Amundsen
in France during the war, and Amundsen's first instinct was to
snub the man at once. He was used to people claiming to have
met him and wanting to chatter, timewasters all of them. And
of late worse; he'd had a lot of trouble recently with unwelcome
strangers come to serve summons or dun him for debts. 'Your
business sir?' he demanded gruffly.

In a pleasant soft-spoken voice Ellsworth explained himself.
He'd read of Amundsen's visit and lecture tour in the *New York
Herald Tribune*, as he had his recent articles in the same paper.
He'd also read Amundsen's books and was familiar with his adventures. He was, in short, a fan. But that alone did not account for
his presumption in coming here, he went on to say. He had some
experience of exploring himself, in fact had recently returned
from a mapping survey in the Andes. But perhaps of greater
relevance was the fact that he was a native of New York. This

was his hometown, he knew his way around the city and would be happy, indeed honoured, to be of service during Amundsen's visit. If he happened not to be engaged this evening it would be his pleasure to invite him to dinner.

They ate at a restaurant chosen by Ellsworth where liquor could be had. He was a man in his early forties with crew-cut hair, open face, easy smile and laid-back manner – though he was, as he wrote later, 'shaken and excited' by this meeting with his hero. And, for Amundsen, to dine with an admirer well read in his exploits was congenial. During bankruptcy and his recent ignominies respect was something he'd become unused to.

Was what he had read in the newspaper true, Ellsworth wanted to know. Was it the case that he was planning to fly to the North Pole? Over the meal Amundsen explained the expedition he had planned. He had won the South Pole for Norway thirteen years ago, won it the hard way on foot with sledges and dogs. Now he would achieve the North in the ultimate of modern technology, an aeroplane. To be the first to fly there meant glory to his country, reward and worldwide fame. To fail, once in the air, meant almost certain death. No rescue could reach you in that frozen desolation and there was no way out. But it was Amundsen's intention to try for it and his plans were formed. He would take off from Kings Bay in Spitsbergen, the nearest practicable point to his objective. The round trip to the Pole and back was 1,600 miles.

Ellsworth listened closely to what Amundsen was saying. That non-stop distance required a large fuel load, and it necessitated a big plane to make it, he observed. He had some knowledge of aircraft; he'd trained to fly during the war. He knew that Ford was working on a tri-motor capable of carrying eighteen passengers, not that passengers were wanted on this flight but load capacity was essential and the Ford could be fitted with skis…

No, Amundsen informed him, he was mistaken; the surface

over which he would be flying was broken up, a jumbled mass of pack ice. An aircraft with skis could not land on it, an amphibian was needed. An amphibian could take off and land on both water and snow, even ice if it was smooth. He'd already selected the plane he wanted. More than that, he'd identified and lined up the other components of the expedition: the ship, the base, and key members of his support crew. The attempt on the North Pole was – on paper – prepared. Only one essential thing was lacking: money.

What, Ellsworth enquired, was all this going to cost? It had been a good dinner, an agreeable evening, but the question sounded a warning to Amundsen. What was this fellow's interest? Did he see something in it for himself? Was he – in the phrase of the day – trying to cash in on his racket? Amundsen's relationship with business managers had proved disastrous. His last, with a conman in Seattle, had resulted in his bankruptcy. Yet there was something disarming about Ellsworth, he came over as straightforward and genuine, a square shooter.

Amundsen had calculated the attempt would cost $50–60,000, at least. He'd expected to raise the cash from lecturing and private subscriptions, and also out of a book and newspaper contracts, though these were valueless until he'd succeeded to the Pole. And he'd hoped that money might come from product endorsement in the US. Ellsworth pointed out this would become much easier to obtain if the expedition were American not Norwegian.

No, there was no question of that, Amundsen told him firmly. None. This was a Norwegian expedition, it had to be so. Norway had been an independent country for only twenty years and he, like all his countrymen, was fired by patriotic pride. He'd made a promise to his King that the attempt would be made under the Norwegian flag. To Amundsen, national and personal glory had become the same. He was in the deepest and most desperate of holes and unless he succeeded in this mission he was dead, nevertheless he was undertaking it for Norway. And one thing was for sure – if he didn't achieve it quickly someone else would.

Ellsworth considered, and then he came out with something wonderful for Amundsen to hear. Pure music. He said, 'I am an amateur interested in exploration, and I might be able to supply some money for the expedition.' For Amundsen it was an extraordinary moment, the sun came out. Back in his hotel room after dinner they agreed the deal. Ellsworth would put up $85,000 on condition that he became part of the attempt and make the North Pole flight with Amundsen. But, Ellsworth went on to confess, there was one further problem: Father.

3.

THE BACKER

Byrd and Amundsen, the main characters in this drama, have now both made their appearance on stage and identified themselves to you. Each has stated his intention and specified his goal: to be the first to fly to the North Pole. The two men confront each other in the classic role of rivals. But no contest is simply fought one versus one, without consequences to others. Inevitably a tragedy spills over to involve an additional cast, affecting their lives and sometimes even causing their death.

The first of these is Lincoln Ellsworth. Three months have passed since his meeting with Amundsen and he is seated in his room drafting a cable to his partner in this enterprise, who is now in Italy. Wording the text tactfully, so as not to upset the old explorer, is causing him some difficulty.

Ellsworth's bedroom, on the third floor of the family mansion on Park Avenue, also serves as its owner's study. The furniture is heavy, of varnished wood, traditional in style; there's no hint of Art Deco anywhere. Geographical prints and framed maps hang on the walls, the few books on display look like works of reference. The room is masculine in appearance, no woman has had a hand in its decoration. Even without the clue provided by the high single bed with its mahogany headboard, we know its occupant to be a bachelor.

It is 11 a.m. on a cold winter day and normally Ellsworth would have written this cable downstairs in the morning room or library, but in those areas of the house there is the constant possibility of running into his father. Usually Ellsworth does not mind doing so, he can give as good as he gets, but just now he is feeling slightly... he doesn't admit to it in his memoir where he is reticent about his feelings generally, but the only word for it is *vulnerable*. He is beginning to suspect that some of his father's views on Amundsen just possibly may be correct. It is a most disquieting thought.

Fly to the North Pole? A hundred thousand dollars? Over my dead body! had been his parent's outraged reaction when he'd first approached him. But years of exasperation and practice had taught Ellsworth how to handle the old man. It took days, patience, tact and the propitious moment to win him round. Yet, having done so, he knew his father so well he insisted they sign the agreement for $85,000 with a lawyer present.

Being the son of a rich man is not an easy business. If he is over-indulgent it is damaging to his offspring's character, if stingy it is at times frustrating. And Ellsworth senior, who spent vast sums of money on paintings, furniture, books and a castle in Switzerland, was a real tightwad toward his son. But the youth had left home and made his own way regardless of Father and a sometime inheritance. He'd qualified as a surveyor and engineer, worked in the chilly wilds of Canada, served in the war. But now he was forty-four and looked for a nobler future, to achieve something big while something big still existed to achieve.

Ellsworth's hero in childhood had been the frontier marshall Wyatt Earp – a role model later replaced though never entirely supplanted by Roald Amundsen. As a young man he'd followed Amundsen's adventures, read every word he wrote. And in those writings read Amundsen's admission that as a boy he too had been influenced by a role model, Sir John Franklin: 'Strangely enough the thing ... that appealed to me most strongly was the sufferings he and his men endured. A strange ambition burned in me to endure those same sufferings ... I, too, would suffer in a cause ... in the frozen North on the way to new knowledge in the unpierced unknown.' A rich boy estranged from the rich life and a masochist, Ellsworth wanted to experience the same.

At the present moment Amundsen was in Pisa, Italy, obtaining the aircraft for their projected polar flight. There was a whole history attached to these planes, Ellsworth had come to realise with gathering dismay, but the story had emerged gradually and in bits for Amundsen had not offered it up himself. It seemed that three years before he'd become involved with a business manager in Seattle, a Dane named Hammer. Amundsen described the man as 'a criminal optimist', though when he'd first met him he'd welcomed the relationship. Hammer, a shipbroker, had been very helpful in the repair of Amundsen's boat, the *Maude*, in which he was at that time planning to drift, locked in the ice, across the polar sea from Alaska to Spitsbergen, taking an aeroplane with him to try for the Pole. Hammer's ace skills as a hustler had obtained a large seaplane at no cost from the Junker factory in Berlin, but the aircraft proved unsuitable when fitted with skis. Undeterred, the Dane then came up with an ingenious scheme to finance the transpolar flight. He and Amundsen would design and order thousands of postcards printed on the thinnest paper. People would buy them in order to delight their friends by sending them a personalised greeting card which had been carried for the first time across the North Pole by air. Sold on the plan, Amundsen had cheerfully given Hammer his power of attorney and left him to arrange matters while he himself went to Oslo to persuade the Norwegian government to issue a special commemorative stamp to go on the cards. It took a while for the government to agree but at last they did so, selling Amundsen the entire issue with permission to retail them at whatever price he and Hammer could get.

Amundsen's retelling of this history to Ellsworth was intermittent and in some ways unsatisfactory. Ellsworth suspected that Amundsen himself did not understand the full extent of what the Dane had got up to in his name, but it appeared that the man had then gone to Dornier in Copenhagen and ordered three flying boats at a cost of $40,000 each. He'd put down a nominal deposit – money he'd received from the sale of postcards – and Dornier had proceeded to design and construct the aircraft in Pisa, Italy; the terms of the Peace Treaty meant the company was not allowed to build planes of that size in Germany.

It was two of these amphibians that Amundsen was at this moment inspecting and trying out in Italy, and the cable which Ellsworth is finding hard to compose this winter morning contains a plea that Amundsen should not conclude their purchase until he and Ellsworth are able to discuss the price Dornier is asking. The wording is tricky, for Ellsworth knows well how peremptory and autocratic Amundsen can be if he thinks his decisions are being questioned. Yet Amundsen is on his own admission an inept businessman, and also it would appear a poor judge of character. Ellsworth has an uneasy suspicion other complexities may lie in the explorer's recent past and threaten inconveniently to emerge in the not too distant future.

Ellsworth's cable was never sent. While he was still engaged in drafting it the maid came in bearing a yellow envelope on a silver tray. It was from Pisa. Worded in English but transmitted in Morse by an Italian operator, it took Ellsworth a few moments to decode the scrambled text and realise with dismay that its message was that Amundsen had completed the purchase of two flying boats for $80,000.

By Ellsworth's calculation – and the arithmetic is starkly

simple – that leaves $5,000 to charter and equip a ship, hire a crew, set up a base at the top of the world, and fly to the North Pole. Ellsworth has no capital of his own and there is no way, no way at all he can now go back to Father. He can already hear the old man's derisive jeer, *I told you so!*

4.

ANGELS WANTED

The next scene in this story is set in the north, in a snow-covered landscape impossible to recreate on stage. To continue, it now becomes necessary to adopt the form of a movie and to run the narrative before you as a film. Why not a book, the reader may ask. Because in the course of this story you will come to form an opinion on the characters and ultimately to judge them, praising some and censuring others. Such judgement is not the job of this writer, but for you the reader. And at this early stage in the tale a degree of separation is desirable, a watchful detachment from the players and the action.

It's a bleak landscape that is revealed before us, the habitat of Roald Amundsen. Bleak in appearance but also in mood. He's endured a grim hard-pressed winter and his situation shows no sign of improving. Although he owns, or rather co-owns, two aeroplanes (still in Italy and for the moment safe from the duns), those are *all* he possesses. As before, he is on his uppers. For the moment he still has the house where he waits today – but for how long? Even this is under threat of repossession from his creditors.

It's a wretched afternoon, the air is chill, dank with the smell of tide-wrack. Amundsen's house, located fifty yards from the dark waters of the fjord in a landscape blanketed by snow, resembles a large Swiss chalet with projecting eaves hung with icicles. A stand of silver birch grows beside the building, backed by a forest of fir trees with frosted branches that spreads up the flank of the mountain. There is no colour in the view, the scene could be an engraving in a book of grim Nordic fairy-tales set by the sea. And the interior of the house reinforces the marine association for it is decorated and furnished like a ship, sombrely in dark wood. The main bedroom and dressing room, which form the owner's quarters, are fitted up like a ship's cabin.

In his study beneath the eaves Amundsen stands erect at the window, hands behind his back, waiting. At this moment he is waiting for Major Sverre to arrive with news of the meeting of the Aero Club and how his appeal for funds has been received, but he is used to waiting. That is an explorer's life: bouts of strenuous dangerous activity interspersed by long periods of waiting. Waiting held fast in the ice or, more often, trapped at home waiting for money.

As now. He was in dire straits, the situation was far worse than he'd told Ellsworth. The business with Hammer had turned out very badly. While back in Oslo arranging for the purchase of the commemorative stamps, Amundsen had learned of all sorts of wild stories the man had been telling. Hammer was bragging that he personally had made numerous reconnaissance flights over the pack ice north of Spitsbergen and that he himself would pilot one of the aircraft on the Polar attempt. Total fantasy! Hammer didn't know how to fly and was ignorant as a grocer about aeroplanes and even more ignorant, if that were possible, about navigation. Furthermore, he knew nothing whatever of the Arctic, he'd never even been there. In fury Amundsen had fired him, and booked space in Norwegian and US newspapers to publish the news that he'd severed all connection with Hammer.

A man more experienced in worldly affairs than Amundsen

might have foretold the inevitable result. Every supplier Hammer had dealt with descended on him demanding settlement for the commitments made in Amundsen's name, while Hammer himself fled the consequences, scarpering to Japan.

'To me, to whom business has always been a mystery, the situation was nothing short of appalling,' Amundsen writes. 'I was humiliated beyond my powers to express because Hammer, by making commitments far beyond any resources I could possibly muster, had placed me in a position in the eyes of the world of being a financial scoundrel.'

Creditors presented themselves from all sides. Including, to Amundsen's dismay, his own brother Leon, who had managed his personal business and looked after his earnings since the start of his career in exploration. On the books Amundsen owed him $25,000. Amundsen believed that under normal circumstances Leon would have been happy to let the debt ride until he was able to repay it from writing and lecture fees, but now his brother panicked and tried to recover his money ahead of the other creditors. Amundsen was used to setbacks but this action by his own brother was particularly dispiriting; could *no one* be relied on? Amundsen's only asset was his home, the house in whose study he was waiting at this moment. Leon had demanded it in settlement. On consulting a lawyer (rather late in proceedings), Amundsen learned that this constituted an attempt to defraud the other creditors and, on advice, demanded access to Leon's books. His brother refused to hand them over. There were two choices – either obtain a court order for examination of the accounts or go into bankruptcy. Amundsen chose the second; the court would then sub poena the books and Leon would be forced to produce them.

'I viewed the prospect of public bankruptcy proceedings with inexpressible shame,' Amundsen writes. He'd been respected and honoured in Norway, now he was reduced to penury; barely did he retain a roof over his head. The Norwegian press, which twelve years earlier had welcomed him as a hero after winning the South Pole for his nation, turned and savaged him. He was charged with deviousness, conspiracy and fraud. Amundsen was bewildered, humiliated and hurt by what had happened. After thirty years of arduous labour and endeavour, after a life of the utmost sexual probity devoted to a strict code of honour and dedicated to his country's glory, that this should come down on him was an intolerable humiliation. His good name had been taken from him; he felt mortified and deeply wounded by the ingratitude of his own countrymen. In all Norway only one man had publicly and steadfastly stayed loyal to him: the King. King Haakon's confidence sustained Amundsen; it maintained his troth to his country and his own ideal. Amundsen was a man of extraordinary fortitude. With the weight of these disastrous events bearing down upon him he'd nevertheless found it in himself to summon the will for one final endeavour to redeem his reputation and recoup his fortune. Six months earlier, in a last throw of the dice from an empty hand he had, as we know, sailed to New York to raise the money for a North Pole flight – and met Ellsworth.

Goethe has a poem:

Money gone, something gone
Honour gone, much gone
Courage gone, all gone.

Now, as Amundsen stood at the window of his study looking out at his snow-covered garden and the bleak waters of the fjord while he waited for Major Sverre to arrive with news of the Norwegian Aero Club's decision, he was two down on that list. Money and honour were lost, but courage remained to him. He had a plenitude of courage. And this he knew: through courage, honour and even wealth could be regained, through one last venture on the ice.

In the bleak snow-covered vista revealed from the window, already fading to twilight in the afternoon, Amundsen glimpsed a solitary moving figure. A man on skis, poling with long gliding strides up the lane leading to the house: Major Sverre. Though Amundsen's home was backed by forest and mountains, it stood on the outskirts of Oslo; his visitor had chosen to make the short trip on skis.

The Aero Club of Norway – which had existed only for the last couple of years and had few members – was the brainchild of one of the country's few capitalists, the owner of *Tidens Tegn*, its largest newspaper, but the Club was run by Major Sverre. Knowing Sverre slightly, Amundsen had elected to make his approach for funds through him. Ellsworth's money was already spent on the aeroplanes for the flight. Little remained, nowhere near enough to finance the attempt on the Pole. Ellsworth had made it clear he could come up with no more, and the appeal to the Aero Club – no, not appeal, even *in extremis* Amundsen would never *appeal* for help – his *request* to the Club for further funding was a last recourse. He knew nowhere else to go. He had no great expectation of success. The *Tidens Tegn* had slandered and maligned him along with the rest of the country's papers, and the only reason its owner might consider supporting the polar flight was if he saw some advantage in personal PR and involvement in the news story. Yet Amundsen's heart did not stir with hope as he watched Sverre ski up the track to the house's porch, stop and bend to undo his bindings; nor did his leathery face alter its stern expression even by a flicker.

Never complain, never explain, never apologise. He lived by a rigid code: in failure and success, in prosperity and adversity, he was always the same man. Turning from the window and its empty view, he went downstairs to greet his visitor and learn his news. He did not flinch from Fate. On many occasions he had challenged her, putting his own and the lives of others on the line, to find in those mortal confrontations that Fate backed off – as she did now. For, contrary to what he had imagined, Amundsen heard from Sverre that he had the money. The flight to the Pole could go ahead. He might be bankrupt, discredited and regarded as a has-been, but he was not finished. He was still in the race.

5.

STAGECRAFT

The screen is filled by an image of man-made grandeur, a neo-classical façade of a monumental palace designed mightily to impress with its tall marble columns, architrave, frieze and confident imposition. An imperial sweep of broad white steps ascends to its base – to the portico of the Capitol building in Washington, which opens into the cockpit of worldly power.

Illuminated by spring sunshine a single character, Richard Byrd, is climbing the steps across our view, and although a few distant figures are visible in the background it is he who commands our attention. Dressed in trim Naval uniform and peaked cap fringed with gold, the brass buttons of his tunic catch the light as he ascends that imposing sweep of steps, and the picture he forms is so emblematic it might be an ad for Valour or a brand of Virtue – for no imperfection can be spotted in its composition. While mounting upward Byrd's limp is not detectable.

The reasons why many of his senior officers disliked Byrd varied – he was too individualistic, not a team player, too pushy, too well dressed, too Goddamn southern snooty etc. – but basically their cause was jealousy. He was very capable, he could get things moving because he could *promote*, he possessed an entrepreneurial ability the armed forces do not esteem. What was particularly galling was that he had *access*; his job in Washington as the Navy's liaison officer to Congress was a fine position of influence. Of course it helped that his brother was the respected senator from Virginia. It opened doors, and one of the doors it opened led into the office of the Navy Secretary, who was no longer the man who had denied Byrd's solo transatlantic flight, but Curtis D. Wilbur, appointed by the newly elected President Coolidge. Byrd was after aircraft, and they needed to be for free. Also he wanted the US government's official endorsement of the expedition he was planning. He wanted it to be clear to the nation *that he was representing America*. It was an auspicious moment to pitch such a venture, the nation was in the mood for it. The US was on a roll so hectic it was breathtaking. America's was now the leading economy in the world; the US dominated Europe's markets, and constituted the overriding cultural force around the globe (95 per cent of English-language movies were American, as were three-quarters of all films shown worldwide). The US was flush with cash and brimming with assurance –

confidence in the future was an article of faith. The country had become a capitalist utopia enjoying the highest standard of living ever known; there was much to celebrate. The nation had an urge for self-expression, and the myriad of tabloid newspapers starting up had need of stories to match that expectation. With increasing wealth and leisure, people were demanding more of life. Citizens were shareholders in progress and prosperity, they felt entitled to a slice of this liberty and booty. The nation was in gung-ho mood, and so it seemed was its Navy Secretary.

Wilbur listened closely as Byrd outlined his project: to sail with Captain Bartlett to Etah, the most northerly human outpost on the globe; from there to use aircraft to establish a forward base and refuelling depot still further north; then from that site fly long probes north and north-west into the unknown in search of territory. To Secretary Wilbur, as he had to Edsel Ford, Byrd spoke of undiscovered land which might lie between Alaska and the top of the world and its strategic importance. Who knew what natural resources that frozen territory might contain? Who could guess at its commercial possibilities? Or, even more crucially, its military significance to some future global conflict? In a pitch which subtly evoked greed, fear and hope for glory, those triple springs of human endeavour, he sold the same dream he'd sold to Edsel. And with the same success. He got the three planes he wanted, big Loening amphibians which could land on water, snow or ice, together with crew and a support team from the Navy. Also a ship, the *Peary*. Secretary Wilbur cleared the plan with President Coolidge, who gave it his enthusiastic blessing.

All these elements of materiel and personnel Byrd acquired at no cost to himself. Around an undeclared purpose – his ambition to be first to fly to the North Pole – he had assembled a major Arctic expedition. And, remarkably, the one aspect it occurred to no one to question was its author's capability to lead it. He had no Arctic experience whatever. Though perhaps the deficiency did occur to Secretary Wilbur when later he re-examined in the sober light of day the epic adventure Byrd had represented to him. For Wilbur informed Byrd that he knew of another American expedition preparing to sail for the Arctic with the same intention of discovering new lands. He proposed that Byrd and it join forces.

The expedition he referred to belonged to Professor MacMillan, who had made three journeys to the Arctic in the past decade. This one to Greenland was sponsored by the National Geographic Society but financed by E. F. McDonald, Jnr, a Chicago radio manufacturer and millionaire. A successful tycoon, he was looking for new fields to conquer and the kudos that goes with. He'd spoken of finding a new continent and 'blazing a land trail across a frozen Sahara', for the expedition planned to employ the traditional method of travel, using sledges and dogs.

Byrd found it politic to go along with the Navy Secretary's suggestion to join forces with the expedition, for he had need of the promised aircraft and the *Peary*, but he must have had misgivings. His agreement entailed an awkward consequence for he now had to dump his eager associate Captain Bartlett from the game; he and his ship were no longer wanted. Byrd informed him of the fact. Exploration for all its heroic aura is a pragmatic business, and the desired end justifies all betrayals.

Right from the start there were problems over Byrd's status and position in the combined operation. The matter was solved by the suggestion of the Navy Secretary: it was to be MacMillan's expedition, McDonald would be second-in-command, the Navy group and their aeroplanes would be under Byrd's control. His orders were to give 'such co-operation, not interfering with the accomplishments of the mission, as may be desirable in the interests of science, or in an emergency'.

In other words the issue was fudged not solved, and the uneasy compromise over Byrd's position would later prove ruinous, but now the joint expedition had official blessing and Byrd could proceed to select his crew and make ready the aircraft for the purpose he intended.

Keenly aware that in Amundsen he had competition in his flight to reach the Pole, Byrd worked intensively throughout that spring, and by the start of May preparations for the MacMillan–Byrd Expedition were well advanced.

The plan was for its two ships to sail from Wincasset, Maine, for the Arctic on 15 June. The three Loening flying boats would travel on board the SS *Peary* with Byrd and his team of pilots and mechanics. The SS *Bowdain* would transport Professor MacMillan and McDonald, together with their party of scientists and archaeologists. The intention was to go first to Labrador, where the MacMillan–McDonald group planned to examine the remains of early Norse settlements, then cross Davis Strait to east Greenland and continue the investigation of prehistoric ruins in an attempt to trace and date the country's original European colonisers. From there the two ships would sail across Baffin Bay, where they would first encounter ice, then work their way through the broken pack to Etah in north Greenland. Here was where Byrd's work would begin. With the amphibians he intended to search for a protected base further north, from which he would fly sorties to search for Crocker Land, that uncertain country whose mountains Peary had reported seeing twenty years earlier, but which no one had since located. From this base, when weather rendered the attempt possible, Byrd intended to make his dash to reach the Pole.

When US Naval involvement in the expedition had been

announced many in the peacetime service saw in it an opportunity for themselves. The idea of the Arctic mission sparked the imagination, it promised a daring adventure along with employment, which was looking increasingly precarious within the Navy. A large number of letters arrived on Byrd's desk in Washington. He interviewed the most promising applicants and picked his men, instructing them to apply immediately for leave to join the expedition. His team consisted of a Naval lieutenant and a petty officer (both of whom were experienced pilots), three master machinists, and an aviation mechanic/pilot named Floyd Bennett, a raw-boned country boy of thirty-five who would be of crucial significance to him in the weeks and years to come.

The long flights he planned into the unmapped region of the Arctic would be hazardous. Weather in the far north was unstable and could change swiftly. Precise navigation was of primary importance, for if a plane was forced down in that inaccessible area it would be all but impossible to rescue its crew. But of the several American aircraft of that time the big Loening flying boats were the best suited for the task. The plane's fuselage, which could accommodate five people, was built upon a central float fitted with recessed wheels. It was a cumbersome ugly aircraft but it had a cruising range of one thousand miles – more if carrying additional fuel in place of passengers – and could land on grass, water, snow or ice.

If he should discover Crocker Land or other unknown territory Byrd was well equipped to record its existence. Each of his three amphibians was fitted with the latest photographic gear and mapping cameras. Communication between the aircraft and with their base was vital; these were the early days of radio and he wanted the best available – and here he ran into a difficulty. E. F. McDonald, Jnr, financier to this expedition, had amassed his recent fortune through manufacturing and selling radios, a business that was booming. He saw the venture as a promotional shop window for his own range of goods. He was providing to the expedition a complete set of transmitter/receivers operating on 20-, 40-, 80- and 180-metre bands. Byrd was accustomed to the longwave equipment used by the Navy. McDonald's sets were unfamiliar to him and he ran stringent tests of their efficiency. The results were unsatisfactory. Determining not to use them aboard the flying boats, he ordered the latest equipment from the Navy. He informed the Naval Secretary of his reasons for doing so, but deliberately held back from mentioning the matter to his two partners in the expedition.

He was at his desk in Washington one afternoon drafting a press release when he heard the sound of raised voices in the outer office. Then the door banged open and he looked up to see a bulky middle-aged man in a crumpled seersucker suit push his way in past his secretary who was twittering in affront.

'Byrd, I want a word with you, jerk!' McDonald announced. He had learned about Byrd's order for different equipment and was sore as hell. His cheeks were flushed and his small eyes bloodshot and angry. He planted his large body squarely before Byrd's desk and hit on him hard. How *dare* he act as he had?

Byrd, cool in white summer uniform, attempted to reason with him, explaining that where they were headed in the far north lay in the auroral band, an area where radio reception was notoriously lousy. They would be operating there in 24-hour daylight, when radio waves invariably suffer greater interference than at night. McDonald could install whatever equipment he wished aboard the two ships, but on the aeroplanes he must have the Naval gear he knew and trusted.

Put a sock in it, McDonald told him rudely. He was having none of it. Byrd remained firm. His composure and unruffled cool irritated many people, who saw it as superiority, and it enraged McDonald. Vetoing the use of Naval equipment, he insisted that all radio equipment would be *his*.

The matter was unresolved and the result was a stand-off but, not for the first time, Byrd had made an enemy – and this one was determined to bring him down.

6.

TRY-OUT

The setting is Kings Bay, Spitsbergen, at the edge of the Arctic. This is a dismal prospect we are looking at, a low snow-covered escarpment raised against a bleak grey sky. The bleached-out shadowless void lacks horizon, definition or movement until a figure muffled in a hooded parka appears in sight on the crest of the ridge, pauses to scan the view and comes tramping down the slope toward us, taking large awkward steps. He is wearing snowshoes strapped to his boots, which resemble ungainly tennis racquets, and he has to swing his legs wide to prevent them knocking against his calves. To walk in them is laborious and Lincoln Ellsworth does not cut a graceful figure as he clumps his way toward us into close-up.

He'd been born a sickly child; puny and undeveloped as a boy, it made his all-achieving father impatient. In adolescence he'd set out deliberately to remake himself; through self-discipline and persistence he'd succeeded. Now as an adult he usually walked eighteen miles a day to keep fit, and when in Manhattan wrestled with a professional in a gym instead of lunch. Here at Kings Bay he'd taken to strapping on snowshoes and tramping in the surrounding mountains for several hours each morning.

Returning from his exercise this afternoon, as he came over the shoulder of land behind the settlement, he could see below him the expedition's two ships at the jetty of the frozen bay and the tin roofs of the mining village which had been his home for the last three weeks. Set in a mountainous snow-covered landscape, the Norwegian coal-mining community had a population of fifty. It was a last outpost of civilisation, though the word hardly applies to the dismal cluster of industrial sheds, store, administrative building and grimy slum of miners' huts defacing the white flank of the mountain which constituted the settlement.

It was a wretched place, but despite its limitations and discomfort – indeed to a degree *because* of these – Ellsworth was delighted to be in Spitsbergen. This was the start point for the Pole, and very often during the last months he had believed he would not make it here. His father had done everything possible to prevent him. James W. Ellsworth Snr was one of America's leading industrialists, who had grown mega-rich on coal. The family mansion in Chicago, where his children were brought up, contained an art gallery, which housed a Rembrandt, and a library whose many volumes numbered one bound in human skin, together with a Gutenberg Bible.

Ellsworth's mother had died when he was eight and his sister Clare five. Their father was constantly away in New York, Montreal or Europe; when in Chicago business occupied his day. 'If I did not have for him the warm affection a son feels toward a less austere and preoccupied father, I at least had an immense respect for him, and a great admiration,' Ellsworth wrote later in his memoirs.

Distinctive in its luxury, the Chicago mansion was a pocket of refinement and culture unusual in the Midwest. When at home, Ellsworth's father entertained widely. Illustrious visitors came to the house, among them architects, artists and poets. Paderewski was an occasional guest, and played for the company after dinner. Ellsworth admits he was a little bored by the music. He was hopeless at school, was dropped from Yale, then by his own choice dropped out of Columbia. To his father he appeared a dunce, but when later engineering and surveying became important to him, he picked up these skills quickly. Ellsworth was raised in an ambience of the arts, culture and European travel – and it did not 'take'. He chose as a role model not Paderewski but Wyatt Earp.

From their earliest childish manifestations, Ellsworth's father had tried to discourage his son's taste for adventure, but the lengths he went to in order to prevent him from joining Amundsen in an attempt to fly to the Pole were outrageous. The promise to subscribe $85,000 to the expedition had been wrung out of him, and when next day the contract was set before him he could not bring himself to sign it. For years he'd been trying to prevent this and now he insisted on a condition. 'Lincoln,' he said, 'If I give you this money will you promise never to touch tobacco again?'

Hardly was the ink dry before he was trying to back out of the commitment. First he sent his lawyer to try sentiment: James Ellsworth was seventy-five, he needed his son by him in the sunset of his life. When that approach failed he ordered the attorney to investigate and discredit Amundsen. That too was unsuccessful, for Ellsworth already knew the worst. His father then sought out Matt Henson, the negro who had accompanied Peary to the Pole, to enquire if a flight there was feasible. 'Absolutely not,' Henson informed him, 'The ice is piled up high like mountains.' Ellsworth's answer to this was to repeat Peary's own prediction that the future of Arctic exploration lay with the aeroplane. His father's next move was to call the State Department, instructing them to cancel his son's passport and restrain him by force.

These were some of the difficulties Ellsworth had to deal with throughout the previous winter while Amundsen was staying at the Waldorf. He had visited him there frequently to discuss their plans; more than once during their meetings he'd heard the rustle of a sheet of paper slid beneath the door: another court summons for Amundsen. They had been anxious weeks and not the best mental preparation for an expedition. In the end it was only the intervention of Clare, Ellsworth's sister, that induced their father to back off. But he did so with bad grace, threatening both his children with disinheritance and refusing to see his son off when finally he sailed from New York to join Amundsen in Norway. Clare did come to wish him goodbye but could not keep from weeping. Choked with tears, she was convinced this was the last time she would see him. It was a dismal parting.

But Ellsworth's sadness did not endure. As the liner was shunted from the pier and moved down river, he realised he was at last free, and we have his own words recording the shift in mood that took place within him.

> Then my depression dropped from me like a cloak. It was a mild March day – the first hint of spring. Spring would soon touch the Arctic too, and there lay my destiny. With a buoyant step I walked forward to watch the passage of the Narrows, *lighting a cigarette as I went…*

⁂

The Amundsen–Ellsworth Expedition (as it was now publicly known) sailed from Norway to Spitsbergen in two ships, neither of them well suited for the stormy 500-mile voyage or the job in hand. The *Hobby* transported the expedition's materiel and supplies, her decks stacked high with huge crates containing the two dismantled flying boats; the ship was top heavy and dangerously overloaded. The *Farm* was the King's yacht, a fragile wooden vessel built for summer pleasure cruising, which had been lent to Amundsen by His Majesty.

Spitsbergen was still in the iron grip of winter. They arrived to find Kings Bay blocked by ice. Not until 16 April could they unload the *Hobby* at the jetty, and manhandle the aeroplane crates over snow and ice up the slope to the settlement's machine shop. There in the open, in unrelenting bad weather, fierce wind and frequent snowstorms, the work of assembling the two Dorniers began.

The expedition's technical crew and support party – which had been housed out with considerable inconvenience and discomfort around the village's primitive buildings – was made up of the two pilots and two mechanics who would fly the planes, a doctor, a pharmacist, a meteorologist, an engineer from Rolls Royce, two newspaper reporters and a movie cameraman/photographer; plus the officers and crew of the two ships which had brought them all here. As Ellsworth trudged down the mountain into the settlement that afternoon of 4 May he saw most of the members of this disparate group gathered around Amundsen outside the machine shop. Beyond them stood the two Dornier Wal amphibians in their cradles, resembling long punts with raised wings on which was set the gross bulk of the fore and aft motor. Their shape was extraordinarily graceless and the impression of Heath Robinson improvisation was reinforced if you knew that part of the standard emergency gear stored in the hull was a mast and sail.

The men outside the machine shop glanced at Ellsworth as he halted beside them. The Norwegians were a taciturn bunch but he sensed something in the air, a tension. Amundsen held up a piece of paper to Ellsworth, a met. report. Weather was breaking up, he announced. Spring was on its way and skies toward the Pole were clearing. They must prepare for take-off.

The Dornier flying boats N24 and N25 were dismounted from their cradles and rested on launching ramps on shore, from which they could slide down onto the ice covering the fjord. Equipment and supplies were already being loaded on board after being carefully weighed. It was evident that each aircraft would be carrying a load some thousand pounds above its rated capacity. 'Rated capacity' meant capacity to lift out of water, but they would be taking off instead from smooth ice. 'No problem,' said Riiser-Larsen, the chief pilot, and the second pilot Dietrichson agreed.

As Ellsworth looked from the window on the morning of the 21 May 1925 he saw the pale Arctic sky was cloudless. Gulls wheeled in the mild air above the frozen fjord, bright-lit by the sun which sparkled iridescent on the glacier at its head. He needed no meteorologist to tell him this was the day. The morning stayed fine, met. reports coming in remained good. At 4 p.m. the two flying boats were slid down onto the ice; it was easy to manhandle them on its slick surface. Both were aligned precisely due north on the course they would be flying and their sun compasses oriented and set in clockwork motion. Mechanics swung the propellers to start the engines, which coughed into life then turned over slowly to warm up.

Amundsen, Ellsworth and the four who would fly with them finished a late lunch in the 'salon' – the settlement's sail repair shop which the expedition had taken over as a mess – and dressed in their heavy flying clothes, over which they put on Arctic parkas and fur hats. Carrying their sunglasses and bulky gloves, they trod clumsily as astronauts down the icy path to the shore.

The crew from the two ships and the whole village was there to watch their departure, gathered in a straggling crowd, the men black and filthy from the mine with a few hooded and cloaked women sheltering behind them, ragged children clinging to their legs. The newsreel cameraman was busy filming the scene as the flyers were helped to buckle on their parachutes. A round of handshakes, then they were hoisted up like stuffed dummies into the open cockpits of the amphibians. Ellsworth writes:

> I don't know how any of the other five felt at that moment,' 'But in me there was not the slightest trace of fear. I know that in that silent throng there were men who never expected to see us again. In New York and Oslo were plenty of people who regarded our flight as stark suicide… Yet if my own pulse quickened then, it was only with elation that at last I had accomplished the ambition of my life.'

The pilots revved their engines to quarter-power and the flying boats glissaded slowly across the ice toward the mouth of the bay. Once on the starting point both planes turned to point up the length of the fjord into the light breeze. Then on the N25 Riiser-Larsen thrust open the twin throttles. With a roar the amphibian skidded away in a blast of snow and splintered ice. Dietrichson allowed a quarter-mile before storming after him in another roar. Halfway down the fjord one then the other aircraft lifted off, clawing their way above the glacier into clear blue sky. The sun flared on their slanted wings as, still climbing, they banked in unison to take their course toward the Pole.

Five months before this, when Amundsen and Ellsworth were sure of his father's $85,000, Amundsen had cabled Riiser-Larsen in Norway inviting him to be chief pilot on the expedition. Though he had never flown in the high Arctic he had considerable experience in Norway; he and Amundsen knew each other well. Riiser-Larsen had chosen Lief Dietrichson, a fellow Naval officer to be the second pilot and, funded by James W. Ellsworth's money, the two men had set off to visit several aircraft factories in Europe to select planes most suitable for the polar attempt. Both claimed to be happy with the two Dornier Wal amphibians which Hammer/Amundsen had ordered built in Pisa in 1923 (and which the factory had been trying to collect on ever since). Their hulls were made of metal rather than wood, so less liable to damage if the plane had to come down on rough or broken ice, and there were no wing-floats to be torn off in a forced landing. But the deciding factor was the shape of the aircraft's nose. Other amphibians had bows pointed like a boat, the Dornier's resembled a toboggan. Instead of pushing the snow aside, it crested it. The plane had three separate open cockpits, each protected only by a raked windshield. The observer sat in the nose, behind him the pilot, last the mechanic beneath the engine pod, directly above his head on the raised wing. The twin 450-horsepower Rolls Royce motors were mounted in tandem. Their props spun in contrary motion; one pulled, one pushed. The thrust they delivered was such that the aircraft could lift twice its own weight, and one engine alone could sustain it in level flight with a full load. Most crucially, it could take off from water even with one motor out of action.

The Pisa plant had carried out a number of modifications on Amundsen's and Riiser-Larsen's instructions: the motors were insulated, a heater was installed to keep the engines warm when the planes were on the ground, runners were bolted along the bottom of the hull so the flying boats would steer straight on ice or snow. They were prepared as far as they could be for the extreme conditions in which they would have to operate.

⁂

The intention of the Amundsen–Ellsworth expedition, which had been agreed with the Aero Club of Norway as a condition of their funding, was to fly to the North Pole, drop a national flag to claim the prize for Norway, then return to Kings Bay. The *secret* intention agreed between Amundsen and Ellsworth was different. Their plan was to land at the Pole and, after taking soundings and observations, to transfer the remaining fuel into one plane, then – abandoning the other – all six cram aboard her and fly on to Alaska. A Europe–America transcontinental flight of more than 3,000 miles: it was an ambitious plan.

After taking off, the Dorniers flew above a fleecy sea of fog for two hours. 'Two gnats in a void of sky and nether mist', as Ellsworth describes the scene.

> Below each ship … travelled a double halo – two perfect wraith-like circles of rainbow with reversed colours – and in the very centre of them the sharp shadow of the plane leaped along the eddies and billows of the fog-roof. It was unreal, mystic, fraught with proph-ecy. Something ahead was hidden and we were going to find it … Now and then I saw down through holes in the fog to the sullen waters of the Arctic Ocean, foaming under a north-east breeze. We huddled down behind our shields, for the wind cut like a knife…

The two amphibians flew abreast at a speed of 75 mph. They were near enough to communicate by hand signals, which was as well, for Ellsworth's plane had no radio. It had failed to arrive in Kings Bay and they'd decided not to wait for one. Other technical equipment aboard the flying boats was, by modern standards *primitive in the extreme*, but state of the art in 1925, for as soon as the Amundsen–Ellsworth expedition had announced its plan they had been besieged by every instrument maker offering his latest inventions. They had gyroscopes for blind flying and specially adapted compasses for use near the magnetic pole, but their prime navigational tool was a sun compass invented by Goerz in Germany. This worked through a periscope in front of the pilot's windshield, rotated by clockwork so it always kept pointing at the sun. Reflectors threw an image of the sun's disc upon a ground-glass dial on the dashboard; so long as the image remained centred on the dial, the pilot was on course. But the instrument did not allow for drift; the aircraft might be merely paralleling its true course although the compass was registering correctly.

After two hours the mist beneath the planes began to dissolve and Ellsworth looked down in awe.

> Abruptly the edge of the fog-bank slipped under our wings and ahead of us spread one of the most sublime spectacles the world could afford – the great frozen North itself … Ahead and to east and west as far as the eye could reach it spread … the sun drew a broad gleaming trail over it. I thought I had never seen anything so beautiful.

They flew on for seven hours over the same vast shining view, which stretched sixty or seventy miles in every direction. Ellsworth's 'shaky observations' with the sextant told him they had reached 'a very high latitude'. They were near to the Pole and very soon must land – but where? Beneath them lay humped and broken ice split by channels of water filled with floating floes.

Suddenly Ellsworth saw the N25 bank and start to spiral down, Amundsen signalling them to follow with a wave of his arm. Dietrichson did so, and from the N24 Ellsworth watched Amundsen's plane descend into a precipitous wasteland:

> I have never looked down upon a more terrifying place in which to land an aeroplane … Great blocks of ice were upended or piled one upon another. Pressure-ridges stood up like fortress walls. The leads that had looked so innocent from aloft proved to be gulches and miniature canyons. In them, amid a chaos of floes and slush ice, floated veritable bergs of old blue Arctic ice.

Amundsen's plane disappeared from sight among the canyons and for another ten minutes Dietrichson flew on, looking for open water. He spotted a lead, but it was choked with ice. Ahead it widened into a small lagoon. He cut the motors. The aircraft lost speed, stalled, and pancaked down hard onto the surface, surging forward on its own wave. In the craft's nose, Ellsworth saw an ice-floe rear up before him. He was flung forward as the bows of the flying boat smashed into it and rode up onto the ice.

In the sudden stillness that followed Ellsworth was aware of a muffled shouting, he was deaf from the roar of the motors. It was Dietrichson yanking on the bell-cord and yelling back to the mechanic, 'Omdal, Omdal, the plane is leaking like hell!' Dazed by the suddenness of what had happened, Ellsworth clambered out of his seat and jumped down onto the ice…

7.

THE FINE ART OF UPSTAGING

Richard Byrd is seated restless and ill at ease in his study in Boston, listening to the radio for news on Amundsen and Ellsworth's polar flight, whose result is crucial to his career. If they succeed in reaching the Pole his years of preparation and the carefully laid plans for his life are rendered valueless, his future is wiped out in that instant.

The Byrds' large family home on Brimmer Street is fashionably stylish; the word people tend to use when describing it is 'elegant'. The American colonial furniture, polished wood floors and fine rugs convey a restrained good taste. Back Bay is one of the best residential areas in Boston, a neighbourhood of substantial well-spaced houses with established gardens and tall trees. Those living here – whose dinner parties the Byrds regularly attend – are bankers, doctors, the partners in family law firms and other well-to-do people who entertain regularly, live comfortable civilised unshowy lives, and mostly go to church on Sundays.

Byrd had grown up in a gracious house; as an adult he'd bought another. This one employs fewer servants – and those Irish rather than black – and unlike his childhood home is equipped with vacuum cleaner, dishwasher, washing machine, refrigerator and every available household appliance. Despite the antique furniture, the place is a showcase of prosperous modernity. Marie has been raised to expect the same high standard of living as himself. 'Elegant' is a word people applied to her as well as to the home she decorated with the full approval of her husband, whose tastes, political views and social attitudes harmoniously twin her own. It is a happy marriage, blessed by three healthy children who all attend private schools. The Byrds' looks to be an enviable family situation of comfortable affluence but, invisible to the eye, the financial basis it rests on is shaky. Even when supplemented by Marie's private income, his service pay is inadequate to sustain this lifestyle and keep up appearances. Aged thirty-seven, he is still only a lieutenant-commander, unlikely ever to gain command of his own ship. Effectively, he waved goodbye to promotion in the Navy when he bypassed his superiors to go directly to the Secretary for authorisation of his previous Arctic expedition; he'd burnt his boats. Yet if the expedition he is about to start on now – particularly the polar flight – is successful, his reputation is made. Success will take care of everything, the future is solved at a stroke.

The two ships of his new MacMillan–Byrd expedition are almost ready to set sail… but yesterday Amundsen and Ellsworth took off from Spitsbergen. If they make it to the Pole Byrd's plan is a wash-out.

On the radio the sound of jazz comes to an end and Byrd leans forward to the freestanding wireless cabinet, tense. A weather report follows, and then the news… the sports news… a market report, cheerfully upbeat. Then another announcer's voice more measured in tone, followed by a concert relayed by NBC from New York. Byrd's attention relaxes. But abruptly the lush music is interrupted for a news flash. The two aircraft of the Amundsen–Ellsworth expedition have failed to make it back to

Spitsbergen. They and their crews are down somewhere on the Arctic ice.

Nowhere in his several books does Byrd hint of his reaction at that moment. Concern for his fellow aviators down, perhaps injured, in a perilous situation must have formed part of it – although surely as a secondary response – but he confides nothing of the relief which must have flooded through him on hearing the news. A rush of exhilaration that the race is still open… and then, a moment later, a further thought, the realisation that in this event fate has dealt him a wild card.

The stature of a hero – call to mind any action adventure movie familiar to you – is defined by the magnitude and difficulty he or she must overcome to win. And in life, which seldom goes quite like a movie, these heroic opportunities (together with the media interest they command) are rare. It is vital to seize them. Byrd can still be first to claim the Pole – but a prior challenge lies to hand.

He calls Professor MacMillan, who has already heard the news. There is, Byrd tells him, only one possible way for them to act now. They must at once load equipment and stores on board their ships and make ready to depart. Ever the consummate PR man, he proposes to issue an immediate press release announcing that the MacMillan–Byrd Expedition is setting aside its own plans and with its three aircraft sailing to the rescue of Amundsen and Ellsworth down somewhere on the Arctic ice…

8.

THE SHOW FOLDS

The prospect is ice, an infinity of heaped slabs of ice, a hostile wilderness of white in the glare of endless day.

For five days after Ellsworth's plane, piloted by Dietrichson with its mechanic Omdal, had come down on it, they remained separated from Amundsen and the other flying boat. Their first action on clambering from the aircraft was to check their position with the sextant. They were disgusted to learn they had flown 22 degrees off course and were still 160 miles from the Pole and down in the middle of nowhere.

While Omdal pumped water from the sinking plane, Ellsworth and Dietrichson climbed an ice hummock and looked for the other plane, but could see no sign of it. Returning to the aircraft they learned from the mechanic that the crash had disabled the front engine, and that he could find no way to repair the leaking hull. Unloading the supplies and equipment aboard, they pitched the tent they'd brought with them, sat on their rolled sleeping-bags and discussed what to do.

Meanwhile, Amundsen and the two with him were less than three miles away in that chaotic wilderness of mangled ice. The afternoon of their second day there Amundsen spotted Ellsworth's group through binoculars. The two parties communicated by

77

semaphoring with flags and over the next three days Amundsen watched their slow and painful progress across the ice to join him. The three started on skis, wearing heavy backpacks and dragging a sledge loaded with a canoe and supplies, but it took them an hour to travel fifty yards. Hauling the sledge through deep snow and over mountainous sharp ridges of ice proved impossible, and they abandoned it, together with its load. Taking what they could carry, they continued on skis. The piled blocks of ice were separated by channels of frozen water; the surface bent under their weight. It split and gave way beneath Dietrichson. From a half-mile away Amundsen heard his scream as he fell into the freezing sea. Then Omdal went through the ice as well. Only the heads of the two men were showing as they clung to the jagged edge while the current swept their bodies beneath the ice. 'I'm gone! I'm gone!' Omdal was shouting hoarsely.

These were fellow Norwegians, men Amundsen knew well and who were his responsibility. Unable to help, he could only watch through field-glasses as Ellsworth crawled over the sagging ice toward them, pushing his skis ahead of him. Dietrichson grabbed one and Ellsworth pulled him to safety then slithered over to Omdal, cut off his pack and hauled him out the water. But the mechanic's hands were lacerated and streaming blood; both men were soaked, freezing and in a bad way when they finally stumbled into Amundsen's camp.

He and his crew were living in the lightless cargo hull of the N25, and the new arrivals moved in to share their cramped quarters. The Dornier had come down here not because Amundsen thought they'd reached the Pole, but because one of the engines had cut out. The mechanic Feucht had now repaired this and the motor was functioning, but the flying boat was frozen immovably into the ice. Five days had effected a shocking change in Amundsen. His manner remained calm and confident as ever but the strain showed in his face; to Ellsworth, he seemed to have aged ten years. The situation was grave. The radio was out of action and, even if they could report their position, there was no hope of rescue for no one could reach them. They were down on a vast broken mass of floating ice and the nearest land was 400 miles away. And even if they did make it to the desolate, uninhabited coast of north Greenland, what then? No one cared to raise that point.

Each of the downed aircraft carried a collapsible canoe, a sledge, tent, skis, rucksacks, cooking equipment, maps, firearms (a shotgun, rifle and automatic pistol) and a month's supply of food. But that food would barely be sufficient for the long journey, and only if they started on it very soon. On the other hand, if they remained with the aircraft a lead might open in the ice which would allow it to take off; they might find a strip of smooth ice or frozen snow, or they might just be able to level and clear a runway. Stay or go – that was the choice.

By the day Ellsworth and the crew of the N24 succeeded in joining up with him, Amundsen had imposed an orderly routine on the camp, with fixed hours for meals, work and sleep. Now he put everyone on a ration of half a pound of food per day and announced that they would make every effort to free the Dornier and get it into the air. If they didn't succeed by 15 June each man could decide for himself whether to stay with the plane or attempt to walk to Greenland. 'It will be a strenuous trip but it can be done,' he noted in his diary.

Amundsen's fierce will broke the apathy that had fallen on them with the understanding of their situation. Under his command they set to work. Lashing knives to their ski poles and with a small axe they chipped away the ice gripping the plane and rocked it free. Riiser-Larsen started the motors and, with the others pushing and heaving, managed to urge the flying boat out of the water onto a floe. They rested, crushed in a human mound in the cargo hold. Next day they tried to take off on a newly frozen lead, but the aircraft broke through the surface. They tried to clear the way ahead with their wretched tools but as soon as they did so the floes drifted back to obstruct it. Retreating to the aircraft, they grouped around it, continually breaking up the ice as it formed about the hull to prevent it becoming trapped.

The work continued for three weeks. Driven on by Amundsen, they became automatons. They laboured, bolted a few mouthfuls of food, slept, woke and resumed working in the unending daylight of Arctic summer. They had no sense of time, nothing marked the transition of one day to the next. They were 'pocketed like rats in a trap', Ellsworth noted. He confessed to feeling 'a sort of blessed apathy' about their situation, but Feucht the mechanic succumbed to it and fell into a mood of black despondency. In a state almost of catatonia he stood leaning on his ski pole and watched the others while they worked, the very image of defeat. They became furiously irritated by him, and with each other. The work made them thirsty, but Amundsen refused to drink water and thus infuriated the rest. Amundsen complained Ellsworth's deep sighing while he slept kept him awake. They lived in their clothes day and night, their hair became matted, they never bathed, didn't shave and seldom washed. When Feucht developed an abscessed tooth and swollen jaw they could muster little sympathy until they found the poor fellow leaning against the plane's hull while he tried to extract it with a monkey wrench. Then one man held him and another grasped his head while Riiser-Larsen took the tool in his enormous hands and tore the tooth out.

They located a large relatively level floe half a mile away, but the route was barred by a fifteen-foot pressure ridge of solid ice. On hands and knees, in vile weather, with only a single axe, knives and an ice-anchor they chopped a way through it. Amundsen calculated that, during the whole period they were there, they moved 300 tons of ice and snow. In the following days they stamped down the snow to construct a runway 450 yards long. They made two attempts to take off from it but each time the plane sank down into the surface. On the morning of 15 June, their twenty-fifth day on the ice, Amundsen and Riiser-Larsen got up early to inspect the runway. They found the surface frozen hard, a tractor would not have dented it. Hurrying back to the aircraft they woke everyone up, and Riiser-Larsen started the primus to boil chocolate. On Amundsen's orders they off-loaded the plane, dumping half their remaining food, canoes, sledges, skis, two expensive movie cameras, firearms, binoculars, heavy clothes and even their boots. Wearing only moccasins, they manhandled the plane to face the wind and piled aboard. Amundsen took the co-pilot's seat next to Riiser-Larsen.

In the hazy light the runway ahead was picked out by dark objects, the possessions they had discarded. All braced themselves as the pilot opened the throttles and the engines roared just above their heads. The hull began to move, scratching, grating, screeching on the ice, rivets ripping off as the aircraft gained speed and began to bump – huge bumps, wider and wider spaced, lunging forward and thudding down to bounce again… until suddenly they were airborne.

> I believe I have asked God for help a thousand times during these weeks, and … I firmly and surely am of the opinion that He reached out His hand to us… (Amundsen's diary)

The N25 almost made it to Spitsbergen when the elevators jammed. With great skill Riiser-Larsen brought it down on the sea and they taxied through the waves toward the coast until they spotted a ship. But the crew of the sealing vessel did not see them as they were chasing a wounded walrus. So the N25 had to pursue the ship, wallowing across the troughs at speed until someone on the sealer glanced around to spy them. 'They received us with every manifestation of joy,' Ellsworth records. The flyers secured the aircraft on land to be recovered afterward, and sailed on in the sealer, arriving back at their base in Kings Bay three days later. Their attempt to reach the Pole had failed, but they had survived it.

9.

FAT EXTRA BRINGS DOWN THE CURTAIN

In a fair breeze under a sunny sky the two ships of the MacMillan–McDonald–Byrd Expedition set sail for Greenland from the US Navy Yard at Charleston, Virginia, two days after Amundsen and Ellsworth are reported safe in Spitsbergen. With no cause now to attempt the flyers' rescue, the expedition can resume its original purpose – together with Commander Byrd's to reach the Pole, which lay within that plan.

The *Peary* and *Bowdain* forced their way through the pack ice to reach Etah in north-west Greenland on 1 August. The sections of the aircraft were off-loaded from the *Peary*, and the three Loening amphibians, NA1, 2 and 3, assembled on shore and then moored to buoys off the beach. The Naval longwave radios Byrd had insisted on were installed and tested, as were McDonald's shortwave sets. In an uneasy compromise it had been agreed that the former would be used while the planes were in the air, the latter when on the ground. Relations between Byrd and McDonald were strained. As he'd threatened, the Chicagoan had seized every opportunity to cause Byrd problems. Twice he had prevented the service radios from being loaded aboard the

Peary. It had taken a cable from the Naval Secretary to settle the matter. The two men were barely on speaking terms.

As expected, radio transmission at this high latitude was poor and subject to interference. Fall-back emergency methods of communication were also tested. The expedition had brought with them ten carrier pigeons. After a week's feeding and orientation in Etah they were taken some miles away and released separately on trial flights. But Arctic falcons cruising the upper air in predatory surveillance targeted these plump messengers dutifully hurrying home and hurtled down upon them, striking and killing six before they could make it back.

On 8 August Byrd flew with two planes to look for a suitable site to establish a forward base. The amphibians' take-off was attended by an unusual hazard, for the aircraft were attacked by a herd of walrus which the pilots escaped only by gunning the engines hard. Their search for a base was unsuccessful as the churned ice was nowhere suitable for landing, and aerial navigation proved even more complex than Byrd had imagined. Compass needles swung wildly in an erratic arc, the instruments were useless this close to the magnetic pole. The sun compass worked, but the sun could not be relied upon to remain visible.

During the following days all three planes flew further reconnaissance missions but failed to locate a landing site. Then in the night a storm blew up and the NA2 began to fill with water and sink at her mooring. After frantic efforts she was attached to the *Peary*'s hoist and lifted aboard, but the aircraft never flew again. The storms continued, but whenever weather permitted Byrd tried again with his two remaining planes. Only after several attempts did they find open water and succeed in setting up an advance base at Flagler Fjord. Mooring the amphibians off the beach, they waded ashore carrying 200 pounds of food and 100 gallons of gasoline, together with oil and cooking equipment.

Establishing this ill-supplied depot behind the beach, they flew back to Etah.

On the night of 17 August disaster struck. Gasoline leaked from one of the fuel drums on board the *Peary*, spilling into the sea. Surrounding the NA3, which was moored in the shelter of the vessel, it somehow ignited and the plane caught fire. The aircraft was cut loose and set adrift to prevent it setting light to the ship. With rash courage its pilot leapt aboard the burning plane clutching a fire extinguisher and managed to save the fuselage, but the wings were ruined.

Only the NA1 still remained operative, the plane in which Byrd flew as navigator with his pilot/mechanic Floyd Bennett. Aboard the *Peary* on the way here and during the missions they'd made together since arriving in Etah, Byrd had gained increasing confidence in the man he'd chosen to be his pilot in his planned dash to the Pole. Two years younger than himself, Bennett had left the family farm in early adolescence to enrol in mechanics' school, then managed a garage until enlisting in the Navy, where he'd learned to fly. Laconic, undemonstrative, dependable, his origins and personality contrasted markedly with Byrd's, yet the two understood one another in all that mattered. They trusted each other.

At the end of every day Byrd sent the Naval Secretary a report on his activity. These cables to Washington were transmitted in cypher on shortwave from the radio cabin on the *Bowdain*, often under the sardonic eye of McDonald, for this was also his office. Time was now crucial for an attempt on the Pole. In Etah the temperature dropped below freezing at night; the sun remained low in the sky, and winter would return at the start of September. Byrd found the delays deeply frustrating as did all the Naval group aboard the *Peary*. On the *Bowdain* Professor MacMillan and McDonald – particularly the latter – were impatient with the flyers' setbacks. They had completed their scientific work and wanted to sail south before becoming iced in for the winter.

By 30 August a new set of wings had been fitted to the NA3. The weather was fine and, while Byrd and Bennett watched from the deck of the *Peary*, the pilot took it up on a test flight. From the deck it looked good, but when the pilot landed he said the aircraft wasn't handling right. It was intensely disappointing for the two to hear. The wind had dropped and the sky was pale blue with not a cloud in sight; flying conditions were perfect for the Pole. Byrd and Bennett each knew what the other was thinking. They could go for it. They could go for it this very moment.

Byrd crossed to the *Bowdain* to inform Professor MacMillan – who listened to what he had to say then gave it to him full on. They'd been stuck in this Godforsaken spot for Byrd's convenience, kept here for almost three weeks waiting for him to mount the promised flights – and with what result? Two planes wrecked and a single inadequate fuel depot less than one hundred miles from base. Airplanes had proved useless in the Arctic, MacMillan stated. There was nowhere for them to land and they couldn't operate in the prevailing weather. He'd already radioed to the Naval Secretary to say so, informing him that the expedition was leaving Etah to sail home – today.

For Byrd the decision was crushing, a door slammed shut in his face. But he contained his anger in front of MacMillan, he was capable of great restraint. He said he wished to send a cable to the Naval Secretary. He drafted one on the spot, explaining the situation and the vital importance of seizing this gap in the weather. He coded the text in the cipher he'd used before, then took the sheet to the ship's radio cabin where he found McDonald seated with the telegraph operator. Laying the paper on the desk, Byrd told the operator to send the message, but it was the other man who snatched it up to read. Which of course he was unable to, because it was in code. But McDonald was well aware of its content: Byrd's plea for delay in their departure so he could launch this final attempt to reach the Pole. It was so little time he was asking for, twenty-four hours would be enough.

At his most needy vulnerable point Byrd had delivered himself into the fat man's hands. And for McDonald it must have been a delicious moment, a revenge more exquisite in cruelty and humiliation than any he could have imagined. He flatly refused to send Byrd's message.

For a few moments Byrd stood rigid as the two glared at each other – and was there a twitch of satisfaction on the fat man's face? Then Byrd wheeled about and strode stiffly out of the radio cabin.

Later on that windless sunny afternoon of optimum flying conditions both ships pulled anchor and the expedition sailed for home.

10.

ENTER FOOL

The scene is a crowded street in Rome, backed by Italian street noise at its most lively and exuberant. But now another discord intrudes upon the usual din and grows in volume as it approaches... The sound of a driver jabbing on his motor horn as he draws near. A new character in this drama is about to come on stage.

There is a place in drama for the Fool; even in tragedy a part exists for him. His role is that of a clown, to subvert the action. Even here, in this loud and strident city, his noisy buffoonery signals his approach. You can hear him coming even before the little upright car speeds around the corner into sight tettering sideways on its narrow wheels, tyres squealing on the cobbles, scattering children and pedestrians who dodge from his headlong path, then turn to shake their fists and shout abuse after the vehicle as it roars away in a fume of blue exhaust. Nobile is an instinctively bad driver. In his recently purchased family saloon he races through the streets of the Eternal City with a small dog perched on his lap, crashing gears, sounding the horn and late for work as usual.

This is our first fleeting glimpse of Umberto Nobile as he dashes across stage in urgent motion as always, but it is characteristic of the man. The start to every day is as loud and chaotic as this one. His young daughter means that start is agitated and inevitably there are other members of the extended family staying in the apartment. Nobile has seven brothers and sisters living in Naples, all married, all with children, and all know there is a free bed in Rome in Umberto's big flat. The place is always crowded and turbulent with the unbuttoned nature of the south, warm and redolent of cooking, garlic and Latin domesticity. He loves it; family, noise and exuberance are life, but by the time he's snatched breakfast and kissed his wife a fond goodbye he is invariably late in starting for the factory. Not that it matters, he is the boss.

As he turns into the entrance to the works in Avenue Giulio Cesare the soldier at the gate springs to the salute. Nobile has not yet quite got used to the gesture and it still gives him a small throb of satisfaction. Pulling up at the administration building, behind which stand the huge hangers in which the airships are constructed, he parks and opens the car's door. At once the little terrier leaps from his lap and races for the entrance. Reaching it she spins around and bounds back to him, barking excitedly. He crouches in welcome and she springs into his outstretched arms. Carrying her, he walks into the building.

Nobile is a small man, slightly built, who like many small men tries to make the very most of his height. His service uniform with its breeches, high boots and peaked cap encircled impressively with gold braid is of great help to him in this. Dressed in civilian clothes he looks rather insignificant. He has dark expressive eyes and a sensitive mouth; at rare moments when his face is in repose it had the anxious sadness of a hungry child but normally, as today, it is vivid with animation. 'Ciao signorina, Ciao signore,' he calls out to those he passes on the way to his office and they greet him respectfully with a smile. He is well liked by people working here, but then he is no authoritarian figure. He was a designer not management, a civilian till he was appointed a colonel only a year ago.

It is true the Factory of Aeronautical Construction is somewhat disorganised and operatic in its operation but it is successful and its hangars all are busy. In each a gang of men are assembling an airship Nobile has designed for the Army or Navy. Airships are a high priority for the new Italy and its charismatic minister for aviation, Benito Mussolini. Militarily and commercially, airships and aeroplanes are considered to be the future.

Nobile admires Il Duce unreservedly. He can see his own future in the new order Mussolini is creating for the country. But exactly where that future lies he is not sure. Hard work, application to his studies and ambition, combined with the fear of letting down his parents who went short to provide his education, have made him what he is: a well-regarded senior technician. But he knows that he is made for more than this, and that he will respond to the call of destiny when it sounds.

Nobile bustles into his outer office and sets Tintina down. She runs at once to his secretary, one of the two women at work here, who pets the little dog, feeding her the expected sweet biscuit. 'The mail is on your desk Colonel,' she tells Nobile. 'And there is a cable. From Norway.' The telegram lies on top of the small pile of correspondence. On picking it up his eyes go first to the signature and the name gives him a small jolt of recognition. He is old enough to remember when Roald Amundsen became world famous by conquering the South Pole. And, because of Nobile's own involvement in aviation, he's followed closely the newspaper reports of Amundsen's adventures with Ellsworth on the pack ice only a few months ago.

The cable, sent from Oslo that morning, enquires whether Colonel Nobile in his capacity as a respected designer and constructor of airships could be available to come to Norway 'for an important and secret conference'. That telegram represents a key moment for the man who had just received it. The wording offers promise, and a thrill of excitement and anticipation runs through Nobile's small frame as he reads its text. He senses a door opening, and through the crack he catches a bright glint of destiny.

That is how it was for Nobile that morning in Rome in the winter of 1925/6, on the day that his life changed. But hindsight has a way of remoulding the past. Thirty-three years later, when he will sit down to record the event for a book, that spin which in the course of time we all put upon our past has worked its effect upon him and he has come to remember the circumstances a little differently. He writes: 'I myself had been thinking for some time about the possibility of using a dirigible to explore the Arctic regions, and I was convinced that, with one of my own ships, it might very well be successful…' After a while he would grow to believe the whole thing was his idea in the first place.

Ten days later Nobile met Amundsen at his house on Bundefjord. Also present were Riiser-Larsen and Dr Rolf Thommessen, newspaper owner and president of the Norwegian Aero Club, who would be handling the administration and finances of the new expedition. The money to mount it was already largely in place. Ellsworth's father had died while he and Amundsen were lost on the ice. Become a rich man, he'd put up $125,000 toward the cost of the flight, which would be to the Pole, then continue to Alaska to complete a Europe–America crossing of 3,400 miles. An airship rather than an aircraft was more suitable for the long flight, Amundsen and Riiser-Larsen had decided. Though slower than a plane, if an engine failed they could land and anchor while it was repaired. An airship could carry a comprehensive range of spare parts, even a replacement engine. An airship was more reliable – and safer.

If the attempt was to take place next spring there was no time to build a specially designed dirigible for the flight, Colonel Nobile informed the group. However, nearing completion in his factory was the latest of the N series he had designed for the Army. Lighter than earlier models, it had a larger load capacity, which could give it the necessary range if extra fuel tanks were fitted. A further advantage to the craft, Nobile went on to tell them with the confidence of an expert, was the fact that it was semi-rigid, safer in gales than an all-rigid version; the airship was the ultimate in design and technology.

Though he missed his family and Tintina, Nobile was pleased as Punch to be here holding the floor. During the last few days in Rome he'd stepped into another world. He'd walked the corridors of power, talked as an equal with government ministers, met Mussolini – unadmittedly only briefly, though during Il Duce's few words he'd looked him in the eye and felt a thrilling bond. And he'd come to Norway as an envoy invested with actual power, come not just to listen but to propose. He'd arrived briefed and well prepared. The Italian government would make a free gift of the airship to Amundsen if the expedition to the Pole flew under the Italian flag.

The proposal had originated with Mussolini and Nobile thought it a fine and generous offer. He was disconcerted that Amundsen took it so amiss. The suggestion made the old fellow angry. There was absolutely *no question* of that, he stated. He'd sailed under the Norwegian flag through the North-West Passage, he'd carried it to the South Pole. This was his last expedition and he was flying with it to the North. It was inconceivable this should be anything but a Norwegian venture. He wished to buy the airship outright, free of all conditions.

Nobile quoted a price of $75,000 (almost $1 million in today's money). Following which he brought up the question of his own fee as pilot. A sum of 40,000 Kroner was agreed (worth $80,000 today). Next day in a second meeting he announced that an attempt on the Pole next May was not possible for him; he was already under contract to pilot a flight in Japan at that date. Addressing himself to Thommessen as treasurer, he asked for and obtained the promise of a further 15,000 Kroner.

In the previous two weeks Nobile had stood in the presence of his idol Mussolini, been charged with a mission, appointed an emissary for Italy, effected a major sale, chiselled himself a fat fee, and landed the job of piloting an airship to the North Pole. For a man who was a skilled designer of dirigibles but had no experience of commanding men, none of the Arctic, and didn't even possess a full flying licence it had been a remarkable ten days' work. And this was just the prologue to the drama in which fate so unexpectedly had cast him. The show itself hadn't even started yet.

The ceremony of handing over the Italian airship to the Amundsen–Ellsworth expedition and renaming her the *Norge* was to be attended by Mussolini and scheduled to be a national event. Amundsen and Ellsworth arrived in Rome three days before, travelling from Oslo via Berlin, where they had only thirteen minutes to change trains. While hurrying from one platform to another, Ellsworth was handed a cable from the Norwegian Aero Club informing him that, unless $25,000 required to insure the airship was immediately available, the Italians were not prepared to transfer its ownership. Without the money no handover could take place.

Thommessen, president of the Club, was already in Rome, staying at the same hotel where they were booked. As soon as they had checked in, he met with them in Amundsen's room. He was as appalled by the unexpected demand as they, and had a concern of his own to impart. Accompanied by Nobile, he had already met Mussolini and agreed with his request that one-third of the airship's crew should be Italian. Thommesen went on to explain Italian national pride was involved in the venture and that it would be expedient 'for political reasons' if Nobile's name featured with their own in the title of the expedition. Only in Italy, he hastened to add, and of course it would in no way affect the command structure; Amundsen was the leader and in full control of the party.

Amundsen listened to what Thommessen was saying with growing displeasure. He himself was bankrupt, he felt bad that Ellsworth would have to be the one who came up with the money required. And then there was the question of renaming the flight the Amundsen–Ellsworth–Nobile expedition, even if it was only for local consumption. He turned in his chair to face Ellsworth. 'You must decide,' he told him, 'For myself I don't care.'

Rather reluctantly Ellsworth agreed. Amundsen shared his irritation. With Thommessen for his weakness in dealing with the Italians, and with Nobile for his brazen chutzpah in upping his own fee. Yet he knew it was not the fellow's tiresome character they were buying but his expertise and professional skills. That he was Italy's top airship specialist was sure, but about his piloting ability Amundsen had for a brief while been less certain.

On an earlier visit to Rome, Nobile had taken him and Riiser-Larsen on a trip to the coast in his car. Amundsen describes it in his biography:

Nobile proved to be a most eccentric chauffeur. So long as we were proceeding on a straight highway he drove steadily at a rational speed. The moment, however, we approached a curve … he would press the accelerator down to the floor, and we would take the blind curve at terrific speed. Halfway round, as I was convulsively tightening my grip on the seat … and shuddering with fear of disaster [he] would seem to realise the danger, and frantically jam his brakes on with all his strength, which, of course … threatened to topple us over. To prevent this, he would then start zigzagging with the front wheels … His whole performance was evidence of his extreme nervousness, erratic nature, and lack of balanced judgement. When Riiser-Larsen and I were alone, I expressed the gravest apprehensions. If, I exclaimed, this is a sample of his disposition on firm ground, it would be madness for us to trust ourselves with him in the air.

Riiser-Larsen's reply astonished me. 'No,' he said, 'That does not follow. Some of the steadiest, coolest aviators I know have exactly this fellow's nervous characteristics. In ordinary life, they strike you as excitable and erratic. But the moment they take to the air – it may be the steadying effect of the stimulation of danger – they are as cool in an emergency as anyone you could imagine.' Riiser-Larsen's explanation seemed plausible, and I accepted his reassurances … Surely, I thought, if he can believe in this man's capacity in the air after this experience, I need not have doubts about it…

Following the meeting with Thommessen in Amundsen's hotel room, Ellsworth sent a cable to his bank in New York ordering the transfer of $25,000 to the Aero Club to settle the insurance problem. The handover ceremony at Ciampino three days later was splendid. The great white dirigible, 106 metres in length, had been manoeuvred out of its hangar and tied down on the launch pad. It's new name, NORGE, had already been painted on its side; now the Italian flag flying from its stern was hauled down and replaced by that of Norway. A huge crowd attended the event. There was a thumping band, the media with flash and movie cameras, and Mussolini accompanied by a large entourage composed of dark-suited men in bowler hats and military officers in dress uniform of breeches, swagger boots and peaked caps larded with gold braid.

A photograph commemorates the occasion. Mussolini standing stage right displays his famous profile looking full left at Amundsen, spruce in a high-buttoned suit, who returns his regard with a smile, clearly pleased at what has been effected. But Nobile has upstaged both of them. Though short in stature, by thrusting himself forward he appears tall as they. Hat pushed back on his head, staring full into camera, a bemused grin is pasted across his face.

The *Norge* was scheduled to take off on 3 April to join Amundsen and Ellsworth in Spitsbergen. 'You will succeed,' Mussolini told him. 'I am sure of it. You will go – and come back victorious!' Nobile was thrilled to hear the words.

He was obliged to remain at home in Rome for a further week before the weather became sufficiently settled for the *Norge* to start upon her scheduled voyage: Pulham, England – Oslo – Stockholm – Helsinki – Leningrad – Spitsbergen. One of Nobile's brothers and his family were staying in the apartment; the place was crowded and turbulent as ever but running a higher emotional temperature than usual because of his imminent departure. When Maria, his eight-year-old daughter, learned where he was going she made him show it to her on a map. She jabbed a small finger on Spitsbergen. 'There, there's nothing in that! You'll get there in a moment,' she told him.

His wife Carlotta was desperately anxious, she could not sleep at night. Two of Nobile's brothers had come to her, pleading that she dissuade him from the venture. 'She had no illusions about the risks I was running,' Nobile writes, 'She knew them all, because I had told her myself … Yet her self-control was so great that she was able, without getting upset, to listen to the advice I gave her about bringing up our daughter in case I did not come back.'

Carlotta and Maria came to Ciampino on the 10th to see him off, and so did his brothers. It was a deeply felt emotionally expressed goodbye. At 9.30 Nobile went on board the *Norge* wearing uniform and carrying Tintina, the little dog warmly dressed in a specially made woollen waistcoat. Two minutes later he gave the signal to start, 'Andiamo!' The crowd of men surrounding the craft let go the mooring ropes and amid the clamour of farewells the airship rose slowly, solemnly into a warm blue sky.

Nobile was on his way. But during the night before his wife had been unable to contain her distress. Impulsively she'd turned on him to cry, 'I won't let you go!'

He must, he told her. *It is for Italy!*

II.

NEW SHOW OPENS TO ACCLAIM

Ever since his return to America aboard the *Peary*, frustrated, angry and humiliated by McDonald, Richard Byrd has utilised his energy, contacts, lobbying skill and considerable organising powers to put together a new attempt upon the Pole. In February 1926 he announces his intention at a press conference. There is no cover story of 'new lands' now, his purpose is overt. His hat is in the ring.

He is working under intense pressure, he knows he has to shift if he is to get there first. Amundsen and Ellsworth are preparing to try for it in an airship, but by now two other competitors have also entered the race for the Pole. The German Professor Hugo Eckener, who has developed and built airships with Count Zeppelin – successfully flying one across the Atlantic only eighteen months ago – is planning an attempt in a giant rigid Zeppelin, seven times larger than the *Norge*. And Hubert Wilkins, an Australian explorer who was with Shackleton in the Antarctic, is currently on his way to Alaska with two single-engined Fokkers and the intention of flying Point Barrow – North Pole – Spitsbergen, the same transcontinental route as Amundsen is projecting but in the other direction.

The race, for this was how it was portrayed by the media

and seen by the public, appealed to the popular imagination. The public loved stunts. Pole-sitting, escaping from chains or a straightjacket underwater, crossing Niagara Falls on a wire, going over in a barrel... such exploits shared a brash look-at-me exhibitionism and formed the lurid entertainment people enjoyed. But a flight to the North Pole held a further epic quality, it was a voyage into the great unknown. The aeroplane possessed an allure that bewitched almost everyone at that time. Radios, movies, gramophones, electrical devices, cars... in a few years these inventions had revolutionised the way people conducted their lives. Faith in technology came close to religious veneration in the US; there was a belief 'the machine' could accomplish literally *anything*.

But flight provided an additional vicarious thrill – danger. The first US postal air service had started in 1919 and the image of the lone flyer battling his way through the storm with the federal bags chimed with the American collective mind. Aviators were pioneering the skies. Now, barely seven years later, only ten of the mail service's original forty pilots were still alive. They were known as the Suicide Club. Air races, exhibitions and displays of stunt flying had continued to grow increasingly popular throughout the country, though one newspaper attributed this only to the crowd's 'savage desire to look upon mangled bodies and hear the sob of expiring life'.

The concept of a race to the Pole was custom-made for the media. The heroic scale of the venture... a cast of rivals with conflicting personalities... the images of the latest planes and airships... the tension of competition which could be counted on to build over weeks toward a dramatic climax... this story would run, it had legs. With due regard for PR Byrd worked the telephone and connections in Washington. By February 1926 he had more than half of the $140,000 he estimated he needed from Edsel Ford, Vincent Astor and Rockefeller, he had product endorsement deals, newspaper, magazine and radio contracts lined up. By March he was sufficiently confident of his funding to ask for official leave of absence from the Navy Secretary. The request was a formality; he enjoyed an excellent relationship with Secretary Wilbur, who had been consistently helpful in assembling the expedition – unlike the service top brass who had scuppered his application for Naval support and done all they could to undermine him.

Byrd had also chosen the two aircraft he wanted. The Ford Motor Company was now involved in aeroplane manufacture and had a suitable tri-motor in preparation, but it wasn't ready yet and he could not wait. Instead he had selected a Curtiss Oriole, named *Richard the Third* after his son Richard Evelyn Byrd III, which would be employed locally in Spitsbergen to scout for landing and take-off sites. His other plane, a big Fokker tri-motor which was the prototype of a new design, would fly to the Pole. It was named the *Jo Ford* after Edsel's daughter.

He had a ship lined up, the steamer *Chantier*, which he'd obtained by pulling strings at the Federal War Shipping Board, who were letting him charter the vessel for a nominal $1 for the year. And meanwhile he had selected his crew and assembled a large support team of eager volunteers who were standing by and raring to go.

On the date the *Chantier* sailed for the Arctic on 5 April money remained a worry, for he was still short of what he needed by more than $20,000, but he had contracts with newspapers and movie rights. If he won the race to the Pole he could earn that much and more – indeed everything his heart desired.

12.

BACKING LOOKS SHAKY

This is the spring of 1926. A deep carpet of snow covers the landscape and the mountains stand as they have ever stood, yet the squalid little mining village of Kings Bay today looks very different to when Ellsworth was last here the year before. A huge hangar and a 130-foot mooring mast now dominate the settlement.

For the last six months a team of thirty Norwegians has been living and working here to construct these. During the winter the expedition's support ship, the *Heimdal*, and another steamer have unloaded 600 cubic metres of timber, 50 tons of metal, and enough cement to provide 200 cubic metres of concrete foundation to anchor hangar and mast against the gales: in all some 2,000 tons of cargo, plus 4,800 hydrogen cylinders weighing a further 800 tons. To move this mass of materiel up the snow-covered slope to the settlement it has been necessary to build a single-track railway.

Apart from the appearance of the place, on arriving here with Amundsen five days ago Ellsworth had received a surprise, or rather two. The first was to come upon a granite monolith erected by the people of Spitsbergen – few and scattered though they were – commemorating their flight of 1925; the second, to learn that a local mountain is now named after him. This is his first public recognition as an explorer and, although too embarrassed to show to Amundsen the degree of his pleasure, it is nevertheless deeply gratifying.

For Ellsworth it is, as the year before, a big relief to have reached this dismal hamlet, where he is helping complete the base to receive the *Norge*. The recent months have been fraught with anxiety, several times the expedition looked like collapsing. In September, Thommessen (its treasurer, president of the Aero Club and newspaper proprietor) released a press statement about the expedition naming Ellsworth as navigator together with Dietrichson (his pilot of the year before). Shortly after this Ellsworth began to suspect something was amiss from the way Amundsen and Thommessen were acting, but he'd only found out afterward that Dietrichson had announced that he wasn't coming if Ellsworth were so titled. The arrangement was 'humbug', he said, Ellsworth couldn't navigate his way out of a wet paper bag. Rather than offend their prime sponsor, Dietrichson had been quietly requested to withdraw from the party.

In December, Thommessen had assured Ellsworth that the

Aero Club's statements to the media would specify that the expedition's leaders were Amundsen and Ellsworth, with Riiser-Larson as second-in-command, and Colonel Nobile commander of the airship. The Club also agreed that the two leaders would provide the newspaper and book accounts of the expedition, yet in January they signed a contract with Nobile authorising him to write the technical aeronautical section of the book. Amundsen – who was in America throughout that winter lecturing to raise money for the flight – was outraged when Ellsworth called to tell him this. It was a piece of brazen effrontery, he said. He was already furious about news relayed to him by Riiser-Larson, who had remained in Rome with Nobile to prepare the *Norge*. It seemed that Nobile had demanded that the crew of the airship, Norwegian as well as Italian, swear a personal oath of allegiance to him as commander. The Norwegians were up in arms at the suggestion and said they were not going unless it was withdrawn. Amundsen explains in his memoirs how he dealt with the matter: 'I rejected this insolent suggestion with indignation and emphatically pointed out to Nobile in plain terms that he was nothing but a hired pilot.'

Interpersonal and other problems had not ceased, even now in Spitsbergen. Shortly after their arrival the Aero Club had cabled to say they urgently required a further $10,000 to cover salaries and bills for materiel. Ellsworth (and Amundsen) was so disgusted by this latest evidence of the Club's mismanagement that he'd considered throwing up the whole expedition and going home. Only the thought that someone else might copy their plans and reach the Pole before they had time to organise another attempt prevented him.

The cost of the venture was escalating out of control and becoming a nightmare: by the end it would total over $500,000 (equivalent to $6 million today). And it was ironic, Ellsworth reflected, that apart from Amundsen's meagre lecture fees, the only income the expedition had generated had come through *him*. Doubtful of Thommesssen's competence, he had himself taken charge of the US story and picture rights, and sold an exclusive to the *New York Times* for an agreed $55,000. The paper had paid the first instalment of the money on signature, but that was long down the hole. The next pressingly needed tranche of $18,000 was due on the *Norge*'s arrival in Leningrad…

13.

CHARADE

The spectacle is one of carnival, centred around a crowded open-air stage. A military band is playing *con brio* and the *Norge* is surrounded by an exultant mob of people.

Resplendent in dress uniform and braided cap, Colonel Umberto Nobile, commander of the airship, gives the order to cast off at the start of his flight to Leningrad on the morning of 10 April 1926.

The crew on board is made up of five Italians and five Norwegians, but the airship also carries two journalists, an English officer present to facilitate the dirigible's landing in England, and a lieutenant from the French Air Ministry in case it is forced by weather to put down while crossing France. Nobile writes in his account of the voyage:

The Norwegians knew nothing about dirigibles ... So I had to instruct and train them. Many thought it dangerous for me to set out without having on board an Italian officer who was used to our dirigibles. Certainly the presence of another expert pilot would have enabled me to rest from time to time ... but I do not regret it. When responsibility is concentrated in a single person ... his attention is sharpened, his decisions are made swiftly and swiftly carried into effect … There were moments when a single instant of indecision would have been fatal.

Nobile had selected his Italian crew from men he knew well among the workforce in the factory.

> They must be hardened against fatigue, indifferent to danger, calm, resolute … I must have the most complete confidence in them and they in turn must have the blindest faith in me, who had prepared the flight *and would now have to lead it.*

The international mix of the crew gave rise to certain difficulties, not the least of which was communication. In the control cabin the official language was English, 'but there were times when English did not suffice to make my orders clear, and then I spoke Italian…' However the *Norge* crossed France without mishap to land at Pulham the following evening. Nobile was glad to meet the Crown Prince of Norway and Sir Samuel Hoare, British Air Minister, who had been waiting there rather a long time for the pleasure of welcoming him. From there they flew to Oslo; on arrival they found the whole city en fête in welcome. The King himself was at the foot of the mooring mast to greet them. That midnight they took off for Leningrad, and ran into fog. At dawn next day, while crossing a wide colourless plain they saw a group of peasants staring up at them. Nobile scribbled a message: 'WHAT COUNTRY IS THIS? FINLAND? IF SO, RAISE YOUR ARMS IN THE AIR,' and threw it down… no one picked it up. Completely lost, they followed a road to an intersection, then descended to read the signpost; they were in Estonia. They reached Gatschina, the airfield outside Leningrad at 6 p.m. Their welcoming committee had been awaiting their arrival since that morning. Snow covered the ground and the temperature was -4°C.

'I was exhausted,' Nobile writes. 'For sixty hours I had been awake, without closing my eyes for a moment ... I could hardly stand. They put me (and Tintina) into a sledge and took me to the Imperial Palace, where I was a guest of the Russian Government...' Throughout his stay Nobile was looked after by an old servant. He fell ill and had to remain in bed for a couple of days. 'How wretched it was to be so far from home, without any of my dear ones near to me!' he says. 'I knew that I should not see them for months, perhaps for years, perhaps never again.'

Colonel Nobile, with his dirigible and crew, were celebrities in Leningrad. 'But I was impatient,' he says. 'I urged them [in Spitsbergen] to concentrate on getting the hangar ready to receive us: I warned Amundsen that I intended to start at the earliest possible moment...'

At Kings Bay a heavy blizzard had brought the work to a standstill. Nobile received a cable from Amundsen proposing their attempt on the Pole be delayed until June. 'I was completely taken aback ... if we were to postpone the flight it would, in my opinion, be equivalent to giving it up.' 'In consequence Amundsen changed his mind again,' Nobile reports.

'On the morning of the 5th May, I said goodbye to the Russian authorities. I ordered the ropes to be let go.' A cry rang out, 'Viva L'Italia!' The soldiers took up the cheer in their powerful voices, 'Viva L'Italia!' Cradling Tintina under his other arm, Nobile threw up his right hand stiffly in salute and the *Norge* rose free while the military band struck up the Italian national anthem.

14.

THE RIVALS MEET ON STAGE

This is Kings Bay, Spitsbergen, the starting line for the polar race. The landscape is deep in snow and the dark waters of the fjord scattered with broken ice floes. Winter still rules here, yet Amundsen, just as much as Ellsworth, is hugely relieved to have reached this unpropitious spot. The discomforts of the shanty-built slum where they are living do not bother him, here stands the gateway to the Pole.

Getting here was arduous. Not on account of physical danger – Amundsen can handle that – but debilitating to the spirit. Most of the autumn and winter he'd passed lecturing in the US on a schedule set up by his agent Lee Keedick. He'd endured weeks of train travel and hotel rooms, same food, same functions, same material, same people. And not so many of those. On the evening he spoke in Carnegie Hall – built to hold thousands – the audience numbered less than 200. After Keedick had taken his percentage and expenses paid, the results of the tour were disappointing. Most of the money had gone on dealing with immediate problems. He'd been so close to ruin he'd had to ask Keedick for an advance of $2,700 to settle a pressing debt. 'I had a court decision go against me, and would have been arrested if they hadn't been paid,' he writes.

Amundsen was mortified that Ellsworth had had to cover the cost of the airship's insurance, and most recently to cough up a further $10,000 to the Aero Club. The expedition required an administrator, but the Club had proved disappointing, even venal in the role; Thommessen and others on the committee had made several quite unnecessary trips to Rome, always putting up at the best hotels. And the weakness they had shown in dealing with Nobile and the Italians was infuriating.

Yet Amundsen and Ellsworth had made it to Spitsbergen and the expedition was in good shape, apart from its inner frictions. The work of putting up the mooring mast and hangar was complete, and the *Norge* was standing by at Leningrad to fly here as soon as the weather improved. Gales had refilled the fjord with broken ice and cloud covered the sky but the season was on the cusp of Arctic spring. It would show in the next few days and, when it did, Amundsen would summon the *Norge* and start for the Pole.

He was in lead position in the line-up for the race – and race it had now unequivocally become. The giant Zeppelin commanded by Professor Eckener was equipped and ready to take off from Germany to head north. That Nansen was chief adviser to its expedition was an uncomfortable thought to Amundsen. Nansen had been his early mentor and benefactor, had lent him a ship. Amundsen regretted bitterly that the man believed he had betrayed him in not informing him he was sailing it south not north. But he'd had no choice. At the bottom of the schism was jealousy; Nansen had coveted the South Pole for himself. Amundsen understood, he knew how disappointment could corrode the soul.

Also lined up on the starting grid was the Australian Hubert Wilkins. The radio operator at Kings Bay had picked up one of his transmissions asking for weather information around the Arctic rim. Amundsen knew he was already positioned at Point

Barrow with his two single-engined Fokkers. He'd be a brave man to attempt the Pole in those vulnerable aircraft, but Amundsen had met him and knew his hardihood and determination. He'd recognised elements of himself in him; Wilkins was a contender.

Since arriving in Kings Bay Amundsen and Ellsworth had been staying as a guest at the house of the mining settlement's superintendent; their support party lodged among the miners and their families in the hamlet's wooden huts. The arrival of the *Heimdal*, the expedition's support ship now moored at the jetty, had added its crew to the Norwegian work party resident here throughout the winter. Engineer Vallini and his mechanics, who had come in the ship, swelled the Italian presence to twenty-four.

Between the national groups there existed a north/south divide: rivalry, incomprehension, exasperation, and a very different taste in food. Circumstances had placed these two tribes together in this outlandish spot where there was no diversion or entertainment of any kind, not even domestic radio, least of all sex, superimposing both intruder groups upon the indigenous inhabitants of miners' families. And now to these three clans occupying the tiny frozen territory in this 1920s ethnological mix was shortly to be added a fourth. Another warring tribe superior in numbers, wealth and technology was about to descend upon them…

A sailor aboard the *Heimdal* was the first to spot it around 10 a.m. His shipmates on deck gathered around him to stare at the smudge on the horizon and the men busy unloading supplies on the jetty below, noticing their stillness, stopped to gaze in the same direction. One of them cupped his hands to his mouth to yell at the mechanics up the mooring mast on shore. The word spread; soon everyone in the settlement had ceased what they were doing and stood watching that plume of smoke far out to sea.

It could be a supply ship for the mining village, it might be a sealer intent on refuelling before heading into the hunting zone among the ice-pack, or… Viewed through binoculars, the vessel appeared on a direct course to Kings Bay. A sense of disquiet, unexpressed but palpable, spread among those observing it.

At noon the ship was clearly visible to the naked eye. The operator came out of the settlement's radio shack, a message in his hand, and hurried through the scattered groups, headed for the house higher up the hill where Amundsen had his headquarters. He told them its content as he went by: the signal was from the approaching ship, the *Chantier*, which carried Commander Richard Byrd and his expedition. Also his plane, ready to fly and with twice the speed of the *Norge* – which had not even arrived here yet. Disquiet crystallised into dismay. The positions on the race's starting grid had changed – and so had the odds on the contestants.

Among the men watching from the shore one turned and nudged another. He too turned, then so did the rest. All looked up the slope of the hill behind them to where a lone figure on skis stood outlined upon its icy crest. He stood straight-backed and tall, leaned forward slightly on his ski sticks, looking intently at the scene below. Raising one hand, slowly he pushed back the visor of his ski cap from his eagle face the better to view the rival expedition. Then, without speaking, Amundsen pivoted on his skis and poled away with long strides back to his headquarters.

By 4 p.m. that afternoon the *Chantier* was in the fjord, pushing her way slowly through the brash ice which filled the bay. Fifty yards from the jetty the ship came to a stop and its captain hailed the *Heimdal*, requesting it to move so the *Chantier* could tie up at the quay to unload.

What happened next set the tone of subsequent press accounts of the competition existing between the two expeditions (for, along with Byrd's support party, the *Chantier* carried reporters, photographers and news cameramen, and from now on every move made by the rival groups would be covered by the media). For it seems that the captain of the *Heimdal* replied that it was not possible to move his vessel from the quay. Not only were they still taking on coal, but the ship's boiler was cold and under repair. The *Heimdal* was powerless to shift over to make room for the newcomer.

So the *Chantier* steamed out into the bay to anchor among the brash ice 300 yards from shore. In the village all pretence of work had ceased. The Norwegians and Italian riggers looked on in silence at the drama unfolding in the fjord. A shift had just come off duty at the mine and the workers in their filthy clothes, faces blackened by coal dust, had joined their women and kids on the shore to watch. Every man with access to binoculars had them to his eyes.

The *Chantier* was seen to be packed with crates – and with people. Its decks were crowded with a mass of them, colourfully dressed and all, almost without exception, staring back at them through binoculars. A boat was lowered, four men came down a ladder and got into it. It was rowed to shore and nosed into the scum of ice rimming the beach. They leapt to solid ground. Their leader waited while the boat was pulled up onto the shingle and secured. He was in Naval uniform, a long overcoat with twin rows of brass buttons, his trousers tucked into rubber sea boots. In his late thirties, his face was very handsome, clean shaven, his dark hair short and carefully combed. While he led his men up the beach it was noticed that he walked with a limp.

The miners and their families pulled back wordlessly to let

the group pass. The only sound was the howling of sledge dogs chained behind the huts. As the group climbed the path into the village they went by the Norwegian/Italian members of the opposing expedition, who studied them in the same hostile silence. A Norwegian Air Force officer named Balchen (who later will play a critical role in this story) stepped out of the machine shop as they passed and the leader of the intruding group addressed him, 'I'm Commander Byrd. Can you tell me where I'll find Captain Amundsen?' Wiping his hands on a ball of cotton waste, Balchen led him and the others up the hill to Amundsen's headquarters.

Dressed in a fur blouson and leather trousers, the explorer was alone in the room, seated at a table spread with maps and charts, and as Byrd was shown in he rose to receive him, his lean hard old man's body crowned by a haughty face attempting a smile. He extended his hand. 'Glad you're here safe, Commander. Welcome to Spitsbergen!' he greeted his opponent.

Byrd was in a furious temper at being refused the quay for the *Chantier* to unload, and Amundsen knew well that he was furious. And Amundsen too was coldly angry over Byrd's presumption at muscling in on the base he had chosen for himself (and was paying for in hard cash to the coaling company). Both had their reputations and their futures, financial as well as professional, staked upon this race. Yet neither betrayed their hostility by so much as a flicker; both were rigidly self-controlled, their manners faultless. The conventions of the period and the code they both subscribed to meant that neither could let his true feelings show. But a deadly subtext underlay their conversation as they unrolled maps and discussed plans and weather. Amundsen was a man of rigid principles, fiercely committed to his honour... yet he was very conscious that his honesty had been questioned in the past. By creditors; in England by the charge that in reaching the South Pole before Scott he'd somehow cheated by using and eating dogs. And by his mentor, Nansen, who believed Amundsen had betrayed him by going south without informing him, *in his ship*.

The Knight may perform no mean or ignoble deed, for in it he forfeits honour. Amundsen was flawlessly polite throughout their exchange, suggesting an area by his house for Byrd's airstrip. 'You are being very generous to a rival,' Byrd remarked, and Amundsen told him, 'We are not competitors, we are collaborators in a joint assault … partners in this venture together.'

Nothing could have been further from the truth – and both men knew it.

15.

FIRST POSITIONS

It is twenty-four hours later at Kings Bay. In his cabin on board the *Chantier*, Byrd is still tense with anger. His two aircraft still lie in the hold with dismounted wings. His ship remains anchored in the bay among the ice, he is unable to unload the planes and get them ashore. Denying him the jetty is a low move on Amundsen's part, he considers. Yet despite his indignation Byrd has not played entirely above board himself. Three months ago, he attended one of Amundsen's lectures in New York and afterwards dined with him and Ellsworth at the Waldorf. During the evening he told them of his own plans for an expedition to the Arctic in the coming summer – but deliberately misled them about his intentions for the Pole. These stories about him trying for it were journalists' fantasies, he informed them. It was unknown lands he was searching for, a new continent to claim for America. He fed them the same line he repeated soon after in a press release: 'The clean sport and adventurous side of this expedition appeals to every man going on it ... The men, all great fellows, are going from a spirit of adventure and patriotism ... We are trying to keep the expedition on a sporting and high plane.'

Well, things had changed now. The *Heimdal*'s refusal to allow him to unload had redefined the rules of contest. It was clear to Byrd that he would be hampered and impeded in every move. The race for the Pole was about to start and the *Heimdal* could maintain the fiction their ship was immobilised for days. Byrd determined to construct a raft and transfer his aeroplane to the beach upon it. It was a bold and dangerous decision, potentially catastrophic, but 'It was either get our personnel and equipment ashore this way or come back to the States ignominious failures,' he writes, going on to express the fear which had preyed on him for months, that if he failed to win this race he would be unable to pay his debts on the attempt and become bankrupt.

A large raft was built by fixing all the *Chantier*'s lifeboats together and decking over them with planks. The expedition's scout plane, the little Curtiss Oriole, was lowered onto it and successfully rowed to shore through the floating ice floes, then manhandled onto the beach. The raft was paddled back to the *Chantier* and secured to the ship's side while the fuselage of the *Jo Ford* was winched down onto the floating platform. As the 74-foot wing was being hoisted from the hold a squall blew up and almost tore it from the grasp of the men holding it before they could tie it down on deck. The wind increased to a 60-mph gale and it began to snow. The raft with its cumbersome precious cargo was moved into the dubious shelter of the ship's lee, but an iceberg now bore down upon them, threatening to crush it. On Byrd's orders, members of his team scrambled onto the berg, drilled holes, into which they stuffed dynamite, and blew it apart.

The gale continued for six hours. Only when it died down could they attach the plane's wing and attempt to scull the raft ashore through the churning ice. When they finally succeeded the Norwegian crew watching the precarious manoeuvre from the *Heimdal* gave them a reluctant cheer of admiration.

While they were engaged in this, other members of Byrd's large support team had been using axes to hack an incline in the shore ice and chop a 200 yard path up to the level ground by Amundsen's headquarters. Now the entire party set to the ropes and for four hours slowly hauled the big plane to the top, using block and tackle. They did so with a will, noisily and enthusiastically. The raucous group was fifty strong, composed of young doctors, lawyers, Naval officers, but mostly college boys. All were dressed in a colourful motley of lumberjack shirts, school sweaters, items of uniform, skating caps, boots or sneakers. All were volunteers, rowdy, exuberant and young. And, recording their efforts were the media who had come with them, reporters, photographers and news cameramen equipped with the quaint movie apparatus of the day. The sombre Norwegians of the rival expedition and the badly clothed miners watched their antics in grim silence.

During the next three days Byrd's party set up a field kitchen by the proposed airfield and manhandled supplies and drums of fuel up the ice slope from the shore – manhandled, because the settlement's only tractor was being used by the Norwegians in their preparations for the arrival of the *Norge*. Meanwhile a massed pack of Byrd's men were engaged in stamping down the deep snow to create an airstrip for the *Jo Ford*, laughing, shouting, ragging and throwing snowballs as they worked, playing up for the media who were photographing and filming everything. 'Not having a level stretch smooth enough for a take-off with a heavy load, we were forced to try another stunt – to take off going downhill,' Byrd writes. 'Smoothing the surface of the take-off runway was the biggest job of all. The men had to work eighteen hours a day, but I never heard a single complaint.'

The weather remained dire, squalls and snowstorms continued, but on 3 May it cleared and a test flight looked possible. The *Jo Ford* was slid from the snow-walled shelter built for her and positioned at the top of the runway. Floyd Bennett took the pilot's seat. The aircraft shot off down the slope with its motors roaring but travelled no more than five yards before a ski and supporting rod broke and it slewed to a stop. The skis were replaced, struts reinforced, and the next day Bennett tried again. With the same result. The following morning he made a further attempt – and another ski snapped. Now they were out of skis.

Amundsen sent Balchen over to ask if he could help. Balchen was a resourceful mechanic/pilot with experience of Arctic conditions and he was of enormous assistance. He suggested larger heavy-duty skis be made for the plane, together with a stouter strutting. The only lengths of seasoned hardwood available were the oars of the *Chantier*'s lifeboats and its captain felt strongly about losing them. Byrd had to intervene to settle the dispute. The oars were planed into skis and fitted to the aircraft. Balchen also suggested that, instead of waxing the skis, Bennett should coat them with a mix of pine tar and resin, then caramelise the confection with a blowtorch. Thanks to his advice the *Jo Ford* took off on a successful test flight of two hours next day.

Without Balchen's technical assistance at this point, and again two days later, it is probable that Byrd and Bennett would never have got off the ground in their attempt on the Pole. One wonders why Amundsen was so very helpful to his adversaries when only days before he had hindered the *Chantier*'s unloading. Balchen has an explanation: 'Practical as ever he admitted to having more than one reason to wish them safely back: should something happen to them, he would have to call off his own expedition and go out searching.' But that is scarcely enough. In his biography of Lincoln Ellsworth, Beekman H. Pool offers another interpretation:

> The Amundsen–Ellsworth Expedition was to be Amundsen's swan song, his farewell claim to glory. No public acrimony should tarnish his name – above all, never again would he suffer the personal guilt that had eroded his South Pole victory over Scott. When Amundsen learned of Scott's fate he told reporters that he would gladly have relinquished any honour or money if that would have saved Scott from his terrible death. But it was too late. Scott had become the hero, Amundsen the villain. Amundsen was haunted by the memory … If anything happened to Byrd as a result of hurrying off unprepared, once again he might be accused by the world of heartlessly allowing a competitor to die…

The history of the 1925–6 air-race for the North Pole is well documented by its contestants in terms of action. But the plot turns on certain hinges which *redirect* that action, and the actual *movement* of those hinges is at times obscured, as the participants, for whatever personal reasons, chose not to reveal their motives when they came to record them. At each of those key instants in the tale's development we know *what* happened, but in some we do not know exactly *how* it happened, and in this case we do not know *why*. Amundsen's reasons for keeping his opponent in the race remain veiled (although we may guess at them from an understanding of his character and past). There are moments in this story about which we can never be entirely sure, and this is the first of them.

On the evening of the *Jo Ford*'s successful test flight Amundsen and Ellsworth were at dinner on the *Heimdal* when Byrd came to announce that the aeroplane's fuel consumption had proved so good that he and Bennett intended to take off in an attempt to reach the Pole as soon as the weather cleared.

'That's alright with us,' said Amundsen with a breezy confidence he did not feel. Only hours before he'd telegraphed to Leningrad instructing the *Norge* to fly to Kings Bay immediately, addressing the message not to Nobile but to Riiser-Larsen: 'For heaven's sake hurry here. Getting awfully sick of this place and all the tension.'

Monitored and reported over the airwaves by the lonely occupants of the weather stations perched around the Arctic rim, weather at the Pole began to clear as a zone of high pressure built up over the area. Temperature remained low but the cloud shredded away in the breeze and the sun shone in the ever-present daylight, glittering on the ice-field. Looking out from Kings Bay across the fjord to the high snow-covered mountains beyond, the sky was a pale and cloudless Arctic blue in which the first glimpse of the airship was a glint of reflected sunlight, resolving into what looked like a silver minnow swimming above the jagged peaks. In the extreme clarity of the light it was hard to judge distance, but as the airship drew closer it became bigger and bigger, a huge monster of a creature approaching with a silent eerie grace. The whole settlement turned out to greet it, for many it was the biggest thing they'd seen in their lives.

The Norwegian/Italian support team formed up in a V. The *Norge* descended slowly toward them, its motors nosing the huge craft into the breeze to hold position. Orders to the ground were shouted through a megaphone in a mix of languages. The mooring ropes were thrown down and a man attached himself to each. A gust of wind caught the airship and they were all lifted bodily off the ground to dangle from the ropes till she resettled. Slowly, ponderously the *Norge* was pulled to earth.

Colonel Umberto Nobile stepped from the gondola in his peaked cap, Tintina in his arms barking noisily. Both were in a highly emotional state, the little terrier at the prospect of urinating on solid ground, Nobile because he'd seen Byrd's Fokker on the snow-covered runway beneath him as he flew in. Spotting Amundsen with Ellsworth among the assembled crowd, he marched straight up to him.

A difficult flight, he announced. Snow, fog, headwinds, in all 5,000 miles and 103 hours of flying time, but he'd completed the long voyage successfully. Slight mechanical problems: a drive shaft had broken in one of the engines and needed to be replaced. He would order his mechanics here to effect the repair while he and his flying crew rested. But there was no time to lose, he told them. Amundsen and Ellsworth must prepare themselves, the *Norge* would be ready in six hours. He intended to start for the Pole at once.

From his superior height Amundsen looked down in silence at the small man before him, who was gesticulating vehemently with his free hand while his other clutched the squirming Tintina. Having eaten his own, he had no sentimental fondness for small dogs; Nobile he regarded with sardonic contempt. 'Nothing doing!' he told him. That weary lecture tour of America last winter had yielded little profit, but it had taught him current slang. Amundsen writes:

> Safe as the journey was ... Nobile grossly mismanaged even that. Besides the necessary foreign pilots taken aboard at Rome to

guide the *Norge* over other lands, Nobile permitted on board a large number of newspaper correspondents, and guests ... One result was ... the wholly needless discomfort of the Norwegian members of the expedition ... Dr. Adam of Berlin had generously made flying suits to measure for every member of the expedition ... At the last moment, Nobile declared they could not be carried because of their weight. Riiser-Larsen, therefore, and the other Norwegians had to make the flight clad in ordinary street clothes. The Italians, however ... appeared on the scene clad in magnificent fur coats and equipped with every other comfort of apparel. Throughout the journey the Norwegians suffered intensely from the cold. Nobile's arrogance and egotism and selfishness were unparalleled in my experience. I shall have later incidents of the same kind to report...

Only a couple of days before the *Norge*'s arrival at the settlement Amundsen's support team had been humping the last of the supplies up to the hangar from the quay. An item they left to the end was an enormous wooden crate weighing two tons addressed to Nobile and stencilled HANDLE WITH CARE! FRAGILE! Halfway up the ice-slope the tractor broke down and they were obliged to haul the crate on a sled the rest of the way to the top. It took them all morning. When finally they got it to the hangar they all hung around exhausted to see what it contained. Inside was a huge searchlight to guide the *Norge* on night landings. Here the sun had not set since 7 April and would not sink below the horizon until 10 September; there *was* no night.

The work of replacing one of the airship's motors and repairing its elevators and rudder took five days. Amundsen records:

During that time the Italians spent their odd hours practising on skis ... They were unbelievably clumsy. None of them could stay on their feet more than a few moments. Nobile fell on smooth ground and could not get up … It is merely amusing to suppose that men of this semi-tropical race, who had not the most rudimentary idea of how to take care of themselves in a cold country, could ever have conceived the notion of undertaking on their own account an expedition which required as its most elementary qualification an ability to survive on the ice in an emergency.

But despite all problems the *Norge* was here in Kings Bay with her flying crew assembled, even if unable to remain upright. Only a short way from the airship's giant hangar Byrd's tri-motor, the *Jo Ford*, stood in her improvised shelter at the top of the runway, her engines kept warm in fireproof canvas bags. In Germany Professor Eckener and Nansen were preparing to start out in their Zeppelin. At Point Barrow Hubert Wilkins with his remaining Fokker (having wrecked the other) was delaying only until the zone of high pressure spread west into Alaska before he took off for the Pole.

The four contestants in the race were lined up on the starting grid and waiting only for the green light to go…

16.

TRIUMPH AND APPLAUSE

A t last, after months and years of preparation, anticipation and false starts, the main event is about to take place. In the radio cabin aboard the *Peary* the shortwave and longwave wireless sets are tuned to the Arctic weather stations and Byrd is waiting there impatiently, already shaved and dressed, when the first morning met. reports come in. They confirm that a high-pressure area has continued to develop and now extends over the whole polar basin. Weather is stable from Spitsbergen clear across to Canada. A light southerly wind is blowing from the Pole and the prospect is excellent – now is the moment.

Just before midday brightly dressed groups of Americans from the *Chantier* climb the hill to gather around the *Jo Ford*, which has been slid from her shelter and stands at the top of a snow ramp sloping down onto the runway. The photographers and movie cameramen are setting up their equipment. Miners with their wives and children stroll down from their huts to swell the crowd, for this is a Sunday and no one is working. Norwegians and Italians of the rival expedition emerge from the *Norge*'s hangar and stand watching as Byrd and Floyd Bennett tramp through the mushy snow to the *Jo Ford*, which swarms with mechanics topping up its fuel tanks and running last-minute checks. The two men pose beside the aircraft wearing fur anoraks with fur hoods over their flying suits, while the photographers obtain their departure shots. Then Bennett climbs the metal steps to the cockpit, waving a hand casually to the crowd. Byrd follows him, pausing at the top to turn and deliver a crisp salute to his support staff before entering the cockpit.

One after another the three motors burst into life. All at once they accelerate in a roar of power. This is the critical moment. The plane shudders, vibrating convulsively, but does not budge. It bucks free, slides down the ramp, and stops. Bennett cuts the engines. He gets out, followed by Byrd, his mouth set tight. They examine the aircraft's skis, and Byrd beckons Balchen from the crowd of onlookers to ask what he reckons. The Norwegian advises to wait till that night, when the sun and temperature will be lower and the slushy surface of the runway turned to ice…

That anyway is how Balchen describes Byrd's aborted take-off. Byrd tells it differently:

We warmed the motors, heated the oil … Bennett and I climbed in, and we were off. Off, but alas, not up. Our load proved too great, the snow too 'bumpy', the friction of the skis too strong a drag. The plane simply would not get into the air. We over-ran the runway at a terrific speed, jolting over snow hummocks and landing in a snowdrift; the plane just missed turning over on her back. A dozen men came up, weary, heartsick and speechless. They had worked almost to the limit of their endurance to give us our chance. I waded through the deep snow to the port landing gear. Great! Both it and the ski were OK. Then I stumbled to the other side and found that they also had withstood the terrible pounding. My apprehension turned to joy …

Finally, at a half-hour past midnight all was in readiness. Bennett and I had had almost no sleep for thirty-six hours, but that did not bother us. We carefully iced the runway so that we could make a faster start … we decided to stake all on getting away – to give the *Jo Ford* full power and full speed – and get off or crash at the end of the runway in the jagged ice. With a total load of nearly 10,000 pounds we raced down the runway, dangerously close to the broken ice at the end. Just when it seemed we must crash into it as we had done before, Bennett, with a mighty pull on the wheel, lifted the plane cleanly into the air, and we were clear at last…

Immediately after the *Jo Ford*'s take-off at 0107 hours the attendant media crowded into the *Chantier*'s radio cabin to file their reports. A release announcing Byrd's start for the Pole was transmitted to US radio stations and onward around the globe. The world waited for further news. Dawn came to the eastern seaboard of America and at home in Boston Marie Byrd and her three children waited near to a radio. As in New York did Nelson Rockefeller and Vincent Astor; in Washington, the Naval Secretary; in Detroit, Edsel and his daughter Jo Ford stayed tuned to the fortunes of the plane that bore her name. No radio reports of either progress, difficulty or disaster were received from the *Jo Ford*. No reports at all.

Byrd and Bennett had taken off just after 1 a.m. on 9 May 1926. The three-engine Fokker was carrying its maximum load, most of this fuel. The rest was made up of survival gear and food supplies, in case they were forced down. They had a tent, a rubber boat, a sledge; also rifles, knives, a primus and smoke bombs. If they *did* crash-land it would be impossible to cross the open sea back to Spitsbergen, they would have to continue on foot across the continent to Etah in west Greenland, trusting to shoot bear or seals for food. Byrd estimated the trek could take them two years.

To achieve the Pole (and back to Spitsbergen) precise navigation was all-important. The *Jo Ford* was equipped with wind-drift indicator, bubble sextant, chronometer, magnetic compass and two sun compasses, one in the nose, the other in the tail. These instruments, together with the flight log, would provide proof they had reached that – till now – theoretical spot at the summit of the globe, which formed the axis on which the world turned.

After lifting off, Bennett took the plane to 2,000 feet, setting it on a ruler-straight course across the map (blank except for coastlines) toward their destination. The distance there and back totalled 1,550 miles.

Byrd provides an account of his epic flight in *Skyward*, published in 1937. After two hours they were over the pack ice, which was cross-crossed by pressure ridges and open leads. The day was cloudless, both sun compasses were functioning smoothly. The plane, which had a hypothetical top speed of 120 mph, was flying at a steady hundred an hour, but for some reason it veered constantly to the right. Moving between the two sun compasses, Byrd corrected Bennett by hand signals. Every few minutes he would lower the drift indicator through the floor hatch to measure the crosswind, but this was a necessarily imprecise calculation.

He looked down on land – or ice – that had never been seen by mortal eyes, his view extended fifty miles in every direction. 'We were opening up unexplored regions at a rate of nearly 10,000 square miles an hour.' He describes 'an extraordinary exhilaration', and 'incomparable satisfaction'. 'I felt repaid for all our toil.'

At 8 a.m., when they were almost a hundred miles short of the Pole, he was aghast to notice a film of oil coating the wing and windshield. The starboard engine was leaking. The cabin was too noisy for conversation. Bennett passed him a note, 'That motor will stop.'

It was a dismaying moment. It seemed the end to all their hopes – and they were so close their objective. The two could not *discuss* the matter, everything had to be communicated in shaky scribbled notes. For the moment the oil pressure was steady, but if the reservoir ran dry the engine would seize, impossible to repair. On the other hand, if the leak came from a loose fuel line, Bennett could fix it if they landed. From this height some of the ice looked deceptively smooth – it might be feasible.

Byrd recalled Amundsen and Ellsworth's experience when they had come down on the pack ice, while he stared at the thin jet of oil spraying the windscreen, freezing as it struck the glass. The leakage was continuous, but slow. They studied it for several minutes, but it did not appear to be growing worse. On the gauge oil pressure stayed firm. Steadying his hand against the vibration of the plane, Byrd noted his decision: CONTINUE.

'At 9.02 a.m., Greenwich time, our calculations showed us to be over the Pole,' Byrd writes. 'The dream of a lifetime had been realised.' They made a circle around the spot, a full circuit around the world, losing then gaining back a whole day in the space of minutes. As Bennett threw the stick over to bank the aircraft, the sun compass Byrd had been using slid off the chart table, fell to the floor and shattered.

At 4.30 that afternoon in Kings Bay, Amundsen and Ellsworth were seated at dinner with their support party when they heard shouts from outside. An Italian burst into the mess crying, 'She come!' All rushed outside. The *Jo Ford* was flying in to circle the village then line up for her approach run. The aircraft touched down at the far end of the runway, slowed and taxied to the snow ramp from which it had set off, where an expectant crowd had congregated. It came to a halt, the cockpit door opened and Byrd

stepped down to the ground, followed by Bennett. His support team, who'd been eating their evening meal aboard the *Chantier*, was still charging up the hill and Amundsen was the first to greet them. Balchen says that he'd never seen him display such emotion. Tears showed in his eyes as he threw his arms around the two men and embraced them, kissing each on the cheek. Then he was swept aside by the breathless scrum of Byrd's party welcoming their leader home, pounding the air in their excitement and cheering his victory. Two pairs of burly men hoisted the flyers on their shoulders and made off with them down the icy slope and the whole mob followed, laughing and shouting with elation as they ran and slipped and skidded towards the *Chantier*.

The word was flashed by radio to a waiting world. At dawn next day the news was headlines in US papers and around the globe. In America Byrd became a national hero, a living legend. On the instant all his debts were solved and he was recognised as a superstar, the revered public figure he would remain for the rest of his life.

ABOVE: Ensign Byrd. Raised in wealth and privilege, from infancy he has been expected to achieve. What drives him now is a consuming desire for fame.

BELOW LEFT: Millionaire's son Lincoln Ellsworth beside the busted Amundsen. 'I'll buy the aircraft and stoke you if I can fly with you.'

BELOW RIGHT: Byrd's rival, Amundsen, Captain Scott's South Pole nemesis. Now bankrupt, dishonoured and hounded by creditors, this race is his last chance to recover his fortune and reputation.

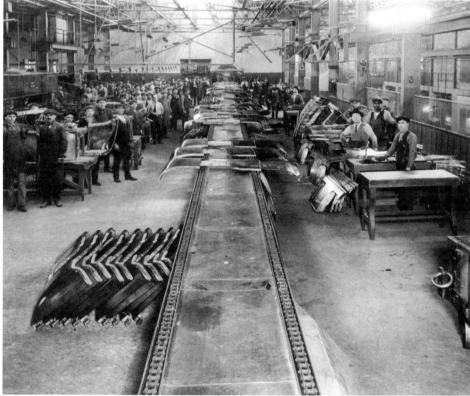

ABOVE: The Twenties. Autos, jazz, movies and mass communication reinvented America. People looked different to how they had before – especially women. They plucked their eyebrows and cropped their hair as short as a boy's. The truly fashionable appeared to be without breasts or waist, to have neither thighs, hips or buttocks.

OPPOSITE ABOVE: Flight symbolised modernity; a plane was the image of the now. There was a plan to build an airport on top of a skyscraper block in mid-town Manhattan.

OPPOSITE BELOW: The River Rouge assembly line.

TOP: First attempt, 1925. Amundsen and Ellsworth down on the ice 130 miles short of the Pole with one plane wrecked and the other trapped in the ice.

BELOW: The race, 1926. Byrd's tri-motor, largest and most advanced aircraft in the world, paid for by Edsel Ford and named after his daughter. Behind it the hangar for the rival Norge.

OPPOSITE ABOVE: Colonel Nobile, Amundsen, Mussolini and Ellsworth at the hand-over ceremony in Rome.

OPPOSITE MIDDLE: Byrd and co-pilot Floyd Bennett just before take-off for the Pole.

OPPOSITE LEFT: Amundsen in the control room of the Norge.

OPPOSITE RIGHT: Losers. Amundsen, Ellsworth and Nobile posing at the end of their transpolar flight of 3,400 miles. By now they are not even on speaking terms – and it will get worse.

TOP LEFT: Fords father and son.

TOP RIGHT: Floyd Bennett and Balchen.

BELOW: La Pas, Canada. The bars, gambling-joints and dance halls of this honky-tonk outpost were throbbing in the hectic fever of a goldrush. Balchen and Bennett relaxed here awhile, as best friends may in such circumstances if they happen to be male.

ABOVE AND BELOW: The start and the end of Colonel Nobile's inglorious over-the-Pole adventure.

Done it! Bennett and Byrd, winners of the race. Byrd becomes the most famous man in America, going on to an acclaimed career. But did he really get to the Pole or was his eminent life built on a fraud that proved fatal to others?

17.

OPERA BUFFO

It is Kings Bay, Spitsbergen, two days later. After round-the-clock work preparing the airship, the *Norge* is ready to take off on her voyage of 3,400 miles over the Pole to Alaska – but nobody shows up to board her. 'I sent to Omdal to tell Amundsen that we would be ready to leave at five,' Nobile writes, 'But four and five went by without anyone turning up. I was tired. It had been a busy day: the sleepless night ... and the impatient waiting had worn me out. Towards six I could stand it no longer. I threw myself down on the floor of the control cabin. Someone passing by covered me with a rug, so that I should not feel the cold...'

Soon after seven the ground crew started to arrive but it was considerably later when Amundsen, Ellsworth, Riiser-Larsen and the other Norwegians turned up with their luggage and climbed on board.

I pointed out to them that now the manoeuvre of bringing the ship out of the hangar had become risky, but that I would try to do it between one gust and another ... I ordered the manoeuvre. There were minutes of suspense. At last I breathed again ... our take-off was assured ... I gave the order to let go the ropes, while they cheered us from the ground ... The weather was magnificent, the sky cloudless. I felt deeply happy, how light I felt! A few hours previously I had been shivering with cold; now I would have liked to take off my furs.

That was Nobile's version, but Amundsen recalled their start rather differently.

I was wakened at six o'clock … Word was brought us that, on account of the wind we should bring with us as little as possible of personal effects. Ellsworth and I, therefore, went … with only what we had on. Imagine our astonishment to find everything about the airship in confusion … Nobile was standing off to one side, apparently in a state of equal confusion … he explained to us that the sun had now risen so far that… the gas had expanded, and he did not venture to start. Suddenly, someone called: 'We're off,' and in a few moments we were in the air.

Later, we learned what had happened. Riiser-Larsen had found Nobile in such a state of nervous excitement as to be incapable of action … Riiser-Larsen had thereupon accepted the responsibility, and … the final swift preparations were made under his orders. The moving pictures, taken of these last moments … show Riiser-Larsen giving the orders and Nobile standing fatuously to one side, doing nothing. Here again Nobile demonstrated his conduct in an emergency. We were to have yet further demonstrations on the flight …

The *Norge* carried sixteen men, ten in the gondola slung beneath her hull, the other six crewing the three pods which held the motors. The airship, which was 348 feet long, carried 6½ tons of gasoline and a further 10½-ton-load of gas cylinders, spare parts, tents, sleeping-bags, snowshoes, skis, rifles, shotguns, ammunition, a large canvas boat and food rations for two months. To reduce the weight, Amundsen had at the last moment dropped three members of the crew, one of them Balchen. Everything not considered essential and all personal possessions were left behind. While lightening the ship Amundsen had been irritated to come upon a large suitcase of Italian dress uniforms, which he had ordered off-loaded.

The *Norge*'s gondola was partitioned into three compartments, with one corner curtained off as a lavatory. There were no seats, crew and occupants squatted on crates or canvas stools, stood or sprawled upon the canvas floor. Nobile, who operated the gas valves, was the only Italian in the gondola. Tintina, dressed in a warm knitted waistcoat, was the sole female on board.

Leaving Spitsbergen behind, the airship headed north over open sea speckled with occasional small ice floes. At a height of 600 feet they flew at 43 mph into a steady headwind, and had travelled for no more than twenty minutes when to their surprise and irritation – for the steady drone of the *Norge*'s motors drowned out the sound of the aircraft – they were overtaken by Byrd and Bennett in the *Jo Ford*. Moving at twice their speed, the Fokker wheeled and swooped around them in the bright air like a swift bird while the Italians grew indignant at the taunting display, but Amundsen and Ellsworth remained tight-lipped… until with a final wave from the cockpit the triumphant Americans turned for home.

An hour later the *Norge* was over the pack ice. 'Everything was working smoothly … The flight went on monotonously, calmly, without anything particular happening,' says Nobile. He told the Norwegian Wisting, who was at the elevator control, that he wanted to take over so he could get the feel and balance of the airship.

Amundsen relates what happened next:

Wisting stood aside and Nobile took the control. Imagine my astonishment to see Nobile standing with his back to the nose of the ship while he turned the wheel around several times in a careless manner. The nose of the Norge tilted downward toward the ice … we were getting closer and closer to the surface. Nobile seemed to be standing in a sort of daze … Another moment and we should be dashed to pieces. Riiser-Larsen sensed the danger, sprang to the wheel himself, thrust Nobile roughly to one side, and himself spun the wheel around. So close was our call it seemed the rear motor could not possibly clear the ice. Fortunately, it did, but it was a matter of inches.

Exactly this same incident happened a second time … Again Riiser-Larsen saw us about to crash and shouted a rough command of warning … Nobile gave a start like a man coming out of a dream. Automatically, he obeyed Riiser-Larsen's command but we barely cleared the ice as the *Norge*, responding to the rudder, rose again. The third incident was this: Flying above the ice, the *Norge* ran into a heavy fog. Nobile spun the wheel in an effort to climb above the fog bank. He was in such nervous haste to do this, however, that he gave no thought to the gas pressure in the bag. We mounted swiftly to a high altitude where the gas pressure inside threatened to burst the bag. Nobile now made a frantic effort to get the nose of the *Norge* pointed downward. The ship did not respond. Then Nobile lost his head completely. With tears streaming down his face, and wringing his hands, he stood screaming: 'Run fast to the bow! Run fast to the bow!' Three of our Norwegians dashed forward on the runway under the bag, and by their weight forced the *Norge*'s nose downward…

Nobile's own account of the polar flight:

More than once my timely intervention served to prevent a catastrophe.

At 1.30 a.m next day the *Norge* reached the Pole. The Italians on board were highly exhilarated, but for Amundsen and Ellsworth to get here brought only a sense of anti-climax. To come second was no cause for celebration, and they marked the occasion drably with toasts of tea.

While the airship cruised slowly over the totemic spot they dropped the small Norwegian and American flags they'd brought with them. It was an empty gesture, for Byrd had already claimed the prize, but they could hardly take them home. Then, says Amundsen, 'Imagine our astonishment to see Nobile dropping over-side not one, but armfuls, of flags.' For a few moments the *Norge* looked like a circus wagon of the skies, with great banners of every shape and hue fluttering down around her. Nobile produced one really huge Italian flag. It was so large he had difficulty in getting it out of the cabin window. There the wind struck it and it stuck to the side of the gondola. 'Fortunately, I have a sense of humour,' Amundsen writes (it has to be said that nowhere in the entire canon of Amundsen's writing is this borne out), 'which I count one of my chief qualifications as an explorer ... It struck me as so grotesque I laughed aloud.'

The *Norge* continued on her voyage, and seventy-two hours after leaving Spitsbergen landed at the tiny settlement of Teller in Alaska. There, some Eskimos thought the airship was the Devil, others a whale, but one man was so certain it was a gigantic flying seal he tried to shoot it down with his rifle. It would have made a fitting end to the preposterous undertaking, but fortunately the Amundsen–Ellsworth expedition was spared that last indignity. They had failed dismally to win the Pole, but they *had* completed an intercontinental crossing of 3,391 miles.

Not that anyone greatly cared – except in Italy, as will be seen.

18.

STRAIGHT MAN SWITCHES CAST

It is two days earlier, in Spitsbergen. When the *Norge* lifted off at Kings Bay at the start of her transpolar flight, among the small crowd made up of its support group, miners' families and Byrd's exultant followers spectating the departure one man stood apart from the throng, his emotions very different from the rest. The Norwegian mechanic/pilot Bernt Balchen watched the airship go with fierce disappointment. Amundsen was an idol to him – a figure both mythic and real, for Balchen had first met him when he was twelve years old. Now he was twenty-seven, a well-built, good-looking fellow with blonde hair, slow voice and easy manner – girls called him a 'hunk'. He was a lieutenant in the Norweigian Navy, but when he'd heard of the grand old man's planned expedition he'd volunteered to join it and obtained leave to do so. He'd worked hard and usefully as a member of the support party, he was scheduled to go on the flight and it was crushing to be rejected at the last moment for reasons of weight.

While standing by the hangar watching the *Norge* grow smaller and smaller till it was no more than a shining dot in the sky, Balchen felt someone nudge his arm. It was Floyd Bennett. The two had got to know each other over the last days and had become friends. 'Commander Byrd would like to speak to you,' Bennett told him. Byrd was in his cabin on the *Chantier*, seated working at his desk. To Balchen he seemed quite different to the man he'd observed before his triumphant flight. All signs of strain had gone from his face. He'd always been handsome but now there was a glow about him. He looked much younger, relaxed, assured, and he was smiling. He stood up to greet the two as they came in. His manner was warm but just now he was the most famous man in the world and he didn't waste any time. He said, 'Lieutenant Balchen, I'm planning another expedition to the Arctic and I can use your experience with skis and cold-weather flying. How about requesting a year's leave of absence and sailing back with us on the *Chantier*?'

Balchen hesitated. He saw that Bennett was grinning and knew the idea had come from him. And Balchen wanted it, he saw a whole new world opening up before him and he wanted it so much that he could taste it. But he knew the code, he knew he had to play it down the line. He said, 'Can I give you my answer in a couple of days, sir? When I know Captain Amundsen has reached Alaska.'

For Balchen this is a decisive moment, for Byrd a fateful choice, for in Balchen he has picked the agent of his own eventual destruction.

19.

FOOL STEALS THE SHOW

The Amundsen–Ellsworth expedition (aka by some as the Amundsen–Ellsworth–Nobile expedition) quits Alaska to sail for home on the old SS *Victoria*, leaving behind the dismantled *Norge* for a shipping company to transport to Italy, where it is hoped the government will buy the airship back. *Very much* hoped by the principals and backers of the misfortunate expedition, for with its failure there is now no possibility its debts can be resolved. The attempt on the Pole has proved a disaster.

Norwegian and Italian members of the airship's crew are travelling together on the crowded steamship. Weather is vile, but that alone is not the reason for an unpleasant trip. By now Amundsen and Ellsworth are no longer on speaking terms with Nobile. In their view he has behaved outrageously during the weeks in Nome, the unprepossessing Alaskan mining 'city' (pop. 1,000) where they waited for the *Victoria*. The two of them and the rest of the expedition put up in rooms rented in private houses. Not Nobile, who insisted that the town's best (seasonal) hotel be opened early so he might stay there. Among the mass of congratulatory cables he received from Italy was one promoting him to the rank of general; lesser accommodation would be undignified, he informed them.

In Nome, Amundsen and Ellsworth, assisted by the journalist Ramm who'd been with them on the *Norge*, sat in a room rented from the local hospital, smoking heavily while they laboriously composed an account of the flight for the *New York Times*. To their dismay the paper was insisting on the 75,000-word piece it had contracted. The problem the three faced in padding out this farcical tale to the length of a full-sized *book* can be imagined.

It occupied them for quite a spell – and meanwhile General Nobile had taken over the town's telegraph office where he was busy replying to his countless telegrams, but more pertinently transmitting his own version of the historic transpolar flight he had commanded to the Italian newspaper *Corriere della Sera*, which ran the piece front page with maximum publicity – then syndicated it to America.

When Amundsen learned of this he went insane with fury. With Ellsworth at his side hurrying to keep up, he strode through the shanty streets of Nome to hunt down Nobile in the telegraph office. Kicking aside the flimsy barricade and pushing through the gang of Italians, he confronted the little general. A stand-up row took place. Amundsen says:

> Nobile … burst into a tirade which revealed fully the schemes and ambitions boiling in his mind. This emotional oration disclosed that he had from the very beginning harboured illusions of great-ness. His vanity, feeding upon his ambition, had built up in his own mind an idea of his importance … When … he grandilo-quently shouted, 'I have given my life to this expedition – *I had the whole responsibility of the flight!*' anger got the best of me. With furious indignation, I reminded him now in no uncertain tones of the pitiable spectacle he would have presented on the Polar ice if the *Norge* had been forced down, and pointed out how preposterous would have been his claims to effective leadership under those conditions. In heated tones I reminded him, for the

last time, that Ellsworth and I were the leaders of the expedition, that we should never recognise his right to claim a major share in its achievement…

⟡

So that was that then and one can well understand that the voyage aboard the *Victoria* to Seattle provided neither a comfortable nor relaxed cruise for its passengers. Both outside and inside the ship the temperature was exceptionally chilly. But on the morning of 27 June the sun was shining as Amundsen and Ellsworth – dressed in the rough suits they'd bought at the miners' store in Nome – stood together on deck as the *Victoria* steamed slowly into Seattle harbour.

A launch sailed out to greet them, flying a large flag. The boat was packed with men and women. As it came closer they heard music. They recognised the melody at the same dismaying moment they identified the flag. The joyful throng were belting out 'O Sole Mio' with full-throated brio. *In Italian!*

Ellsworth writes:

The harbour was black with launches jammed to the gunwales with cheering men, women and children. It was all very flattering and also somewhat perplexing, since when Amundsen and I stepped to the rail to acknowledge the applause nobody seemed to notice us. The bravos from the launches came in periodic waves. Casting our eyes upward at the bridge, we were stunned by the explanation. Nobile stood there, Tintina at his feet barking with excitement. But it was a different Nobile. Despite our agreement to carry no spare baggage in the *Norge*, in his own duffel he had slipped the uniform of an Italian general of the air. Now he was dressed in it, and every time he lifted his arm in the Fascist salute, the huzzas rose from below.

145

Ellsworth's ironic tone hardly conceals the outrage that must have boiled through his and Amundsen's veins as the *Victoria* approached the quay, but there was a final affront yet to come. Nobile had carefully calculated the spot at which the gangplank would be let down and had stationed himself where he could thrust himself forward to lead the expedition off the vessel, but an officer of the *Victoria* had 'sensed this intended impudence and … placed himself in a position to block Nobile's dash for the gangplank, and then bowed to me and Ellsworth to lead the procession'.

A large crowd had gathered to welcome them, including spruced-up officials of city government and photographers. At the very front was a little girl in a party frock with a big bouquet of flowers. Dodging past the officer's defence, Nobile reached the top of the gangplank level with Amundsen and Ellsworth. They pushed down it together. At its foot, the little girl saw three strange men jostling toward her. *Who should get the flowers?* Seeing that two of them were dressed like rough miners but the third glittering and gorgeous in peaked hat, jackboots, resplendent uniform and carrying a dear little doggie, there was *no question* in her mind as to which was most important. She stepped forward and with a charming curtsey presented the flowers to General Nobile, their magnificent leader who had flown them across the Pole.

20.

STANDING OVATION

Meanwhile, three weeks before, another hero has returned in triumph to his native land, coming home victorious on a bright and breezy morning to the best of all possible worlds.

Airplanes swoop low over the ship, dipping their wings in salutation to greet the returning Byrd expedition as the *Chantier* steams through the Verrazano Narrows to enter New York harbour. The vessels it passes are strung with coloured pennants and signal flags, the morning strident with their tooting and shrieking whistles and the scream of gulls. Sunlight flashes on high parabolas of foam from the jets of red fire-boats lined up to receive the explorers home. The welcoming committee comes out to meet them in a tug, its decks crowded with the media. The pier is jammed by a dense mob of well-wishers; the mayor has declared the day a holiday. Commander Byrd walks off the ship dressed in blue and gold Navy uniform. Floyd Bennett follows him, uncomfortable and a little awkward in dark suit and tie. A warm sun lights up the summer day and a brass band is crashing out a triumphant accolade.

Byrd returned a national hero and Bennett his assistant hero, a little bashful in the role. The mayor presented both with the keys to the city. At noon there was a parade up Broadway in their honour, with drum majorettes, marching bands, the fire brigade in burnished helmets and the fifty members of the expedition swaggering proud beneath a fluttering snow of ticker-tape. That afternoon the party moved on to Washington. In the Municipal Auditorium the president of the National Geographic Society announced that Byrd's flight records had been examined and certified by experts, confirming his claim to the Pole. He awarded him the Society's Gold Medal (and also to Bennett, though now and always the spotlight remained on Byrd). President Coolidge presented the medals that night.

It was all so appropriate somehow, so entirely apt. 'Can do' was the buzzword of the 1920s, the faith underpinning the American Dream. It had all happened so quickly, the growth, technological marvels, prosperity and good times had come in such a breathless rush. The modern epoch had burst into spontaneous existence, bringing with it everything – everything, that is, except one thing. What the era did not yet have was a figure to represent the spirit of the age. A pedestal stood vacant.

Byrd's timing was impeccable. There was a demand for symbolic figures, a need created by mass media with its constant requirement to fill radio airtime and the pages of the growing number of tabloids. Mostly it was Hollywood that fed the demand for personal role models, together with sport. Movie idols such as Mary Pickford, Douglas Fairbanks Snr and Rudolph Valentino provided archetypes of beauty, youth and glamour; the Yankees star slugger Babe Ruth – brutish, uncouth and nicknamed 'Niggerlips' – epitomised a macho ideal to many males. And there were business successes like Henry Ford. But a figure to answer the yearning of the imagination for the inspiring, uplifting and incorruptible, an individual who might represent struggle, heroism and the triumph of the human spirit over adversity… as yet no candidate had come forward to step onto the public stage.

America was on a roll with business booming and cash rattling merrily in the tills, but spiritually the country was a wasteland. Despite its sudden wealth – perhaps in part because of it – people had grown disillusioned and cynical. There was little left to believe *in*, what values had not been swept away were tarnished. The war to end wars had failed to do so; it had been followed by labour disputes, strikes, by Bolshevism and the Red Menace, by witch-hunts, race riots and the Ku Klux Klan. Religion was under challenge and the Puritan certainties of the nation's origin had been undermined by scientific progress. The small-town values of God's own country were mocked by writers such as Sinclair Lewis and H. L. Menken, its sexual probity labelled 'inhibition' by Dr Freud. Daily the tabloids exposed a world of sex and scandal, crime, corruption and political graft. In the defiled dark firmament where was the clear light of one bright star? Where was a gentle parfit knight riding to the rescue with a banner of redemption? Where was a seemly hero worthy of the name?

Byrd, who became world famous in a single day, stepped into the flashlights and into a role which had been waiting ready for him. Schools, buildings, streets, ships and awards were named after him, and that winter President Coolidge pinned to his chest the Congressional Medal of Honor, the supreme accolade America can bestow upon its heroes.

He came home a star in a country which was hungry for stars. Receptions and dinners were given for him, he was invited to speak to universities and learned societies, a medal was struck bearing his profile, babies were given his name, he became a myth. In the US not a single newspaper, magazine, radio station or dissenting voice questioned his achievement. In Italy and Norway some did, but this was seen as the carping of small-minded losers and drowned out in worldwide media acclaim. This was a triumph people *wanted* to believe.

Byrd stood for flight, speed, achievement, for modernity. And his plane, the *Jo Ford*, itself became an icon. The aircraft was put on display in New York at Wanamaker's store and the man who stood minding the exhibit was Bernt Balchen, who had accepted the offer Byrd had made him aboard the *Chantier* and was now on the payroll. It was his job to answer the customers' questions and field their comments, one from an elderly lady, 'Tell me young man, how many miles do you get to those tyres?', another from a teenage girl snapping gum to her friend, 'Lookit his big boycep muscles! Ain't he cute, Moitle? Like Francis X Bushman almost!' Exhibited alongside the plane like a prize bull at a country fair, Balchen writhed with embarrassment. 'Of all the things I wanted least in the world, this is it,' he wrote. He so hated the work he was ready to chuck the New World and go home, when the Guggenheim Foundation agreed to finance a tour of the *Jo Ford* around the US. Floyd Bennett and Balchen were the pilots. Starting in Washington, for two months they flew the historic aeroplane around America, covering 9,000 miles and visiting fifty cities. In each the *Jo Ford* was put on public display, in each they were the guests at a municipal banquet where the menu was always Chicken à la King and peas. After which Bennett – and later Balchen – delivered the same set speech written for them by Byrd's publicist.

The two men passed every day together, each night they shared another hotel room. They became best friends. They had much in common, most notably a passion for aeroplanes and flying, but much else as well. Both had a country background and were short on formal schooling; they were utterly unsuited for what they were doing: public speaking. Byrd their absent leader was cut out for the role in which he found himself, they were hopeless in the part. They loathed it, and this created a powerful bond between them. Their incompetence made not a scrap of difference to their reception, they and their aeroplane were illuminated by the spotlight of celebrity and their artless clumsiness was only endearing to their audience.

While they hopped around the country city to city, Balchen sat by Bennett in the cockpit of the *Jo Ford*, navigating, writing up the flight log, and observing the instruments. Every night he worked out the results on a pocket slide-rule. He noted that the plane's speed averaged 70 mph. This was with landing wheels fitted; equipped with skis, as it had been for the polar flight, the speed would have been 3–5 mph less. On these figures it seemed improbable that Byrd had flown the 1,550 miles to the Pole and back in fifteen-and-a-half hours. Of course, if the flyers had had the good fortune of a high tailwind in both directions it was theoretically possible – but Balchen knew from experience that this was unlikely; the wind would have had to back 180° in less than an hour.

So what did Balchen do with his suspicion?

He had good reason not to raise it. He worked for Byrd, his future was built on the man and he didn't want to hear the explanation he suspected. But we do know that at some point, then or later, Balchen *did* speak to Bennett about the *Jo Ford*'s performance, and because of timing and circumstance – the forced intimacy of a shared hotel room – it is likely that it was now. We know this crucial conversation took place but we don't know how the dialogue played.

It is perhaps possible to recover it. A writer composes dialogue from a character's motivation; Balchen and Bennett's exchange maybe can be reconstructed by the same method. Balchen's query was prompted by nagging curiosity, a desire to know the truth, however awkward. And Bennett must have been anticipating it for weeks, as Balchen had come to know the *Jo Ford*'s capability as well as he did himself. At the moment it was asked, each man probably held a drink in his hand, and surely Bennett's immediate reaction was to sober up fast. And then? Did he say, 'Don't ask!'

Did he say, in effect, 'Look we're both of us only hick mechanics but right now we're sitting in the cat-bird seat. We've got a great future with Byrd, don't rock the boat!' And did Bennett then unfluently continue, and grope to explain another reason beyond personal expediency? That if Balchen should pursue this line of questioning it risked not only disgracing Byrd but the scandal would bring shame upon America.

And how did Balchen respond? Or did he not, but instead remain silent, because he knew all Bennett said was undeniable and the reasons to go along with it were both bad and good… for during the last weeks Balchen had looked down daily from the cockpit upon a green and pleasant land of endless opportunity unrolling beneath him and he knew he wanted to make a life in the US.

From this moment on the relationship between Balchen and Bennett, already warm, will grow yet closer, for the two share a secret – and share also the same reason not to divulge it.

21.

LEADING MAN ASSUMES NEW PART

We are in the White House where, in the summer of 1927, the chief executive of the richest and most powerful nation in the world is suffering from a troublesome personal difficulty. President Coolidge's problem is a serious deficiency in charisma. In this new age of mass media, that particular shortcoming matters in a way it never did before. The two preceding presidents had at least *looked* the part. Woodrow Wilson was seen as scholarly and austere; Warren Harding came over as a handsome hail-fellow-well-met glad-hander even while presiding over an administration roiling in wholesale graft. In contrast, Calvin Coolidge is a rhiny, pointy-nosed, prissy-mouthed hick lawyer with a fixed expression described as 'blithe as a mourning card'. Notoriously stingy, he and the First Lady were constantly invited out to dinner in Washington. Painfully shy, he detested these evenings yet accepted every invitation, enduring them in glum silence. A woman guest, observing his discomfort, asked him why he came to them. 'Gotta eat somewhere,' Coolidge told her brusquely. He was so taciturn by nature that it was said that every time he opened his mouth a moth flew out. One of his rare pronouncements, delivered in his sour New England twang, was 'The business of America is business.' Having articulated this creed he sat back and let America get on with it. Believing sincerely that the least government was the best government, he provided a personal example, cutting the duties of the chief executive by 70 per cent, working less than four hours a day and, between meetings, resting with his feet up on the desk. After lunch usually he retired upstairs to his bedroom, though some afternoons he dragged his rocking chair onto the porch of the White House to rock and snooze in full view of Pennsylvania Avenue.

When Will Rogers asked him how he maintained his health and balance in a job which had broken its two previous incumbents, Coolidge answered, 'By avoiding the big problems.' In fact he avoided *all* problems, big and small, and this inertia – dignified as a policy of laissez faire – seeped down to infect the various federal agencies responsible for running America. The country was thriving, enjoying a period of dizzy growth, and no checks, no regulation or restraint were imposed on business which might in any way impede that growth. The unlawful prospered with the lawful, and lushly in the rank marge that lay between. Prohibition had become a joke, nobody observed it. Bootleggers, gangsters and racketeers added a racy tone to the garish spectacle, part of its high-strutting style; mobsters were out there with the rest, foot on the brass rail, wisecracking in a snap-brim hat, cigar in hand.

With prosperity and instalment-buying a vast unity came upon America (except for its farmers, who knew no wealth); a democratisation of fashion and style swept over the country in a conformity of desire. The Sears Roebuck catalogue formed its bible, movies its store window. Clothes, furniture, home interiors, appliances, cars, everyone united in wanting the same things. Consumer values, instant gratification, mass media, the cult of the individual and of celebrity… this was the infancy of our cultural identity today; here we are witnessing our own beginnings.

The era was the golden age of American advertising. Ad revenues quadrupled between 1914 and 1929. Two thousand broadsheet newspapers were published daily in the US, plus another 500 on Sunday, and their huge circulation was dented not at all by the advent of the tabloids – of which there were now three in New York alone – for the tabloids tapped into an entirely new readership. Then radio appeared, and by this date in our story one out of every three people owned a set; virtually every family and every home possessed at least one. Mass media had exploded across America and the country became a gigantic sellers' market. Ad agencies were awash with cash as they orchestrated this bonanza, but not the least of their problems lay in controlling the runaway megalomania of their major clients for – in the same way as today every academic secretly longs to be a media personality – in the mid-Twenties every corporate president had an overweening urge to produce his own radio show. The most notorious of these manic despots, George Washington Hill – president of American Tobacco and sponsor of the Lucky Strike Dance Hour, airing three nights a week – wore a cowboy hat indoors, chewed a gross cigar, shrieked abuse, exposed his parts and selected the bands who would feature on the show by forcing the president of NBC to dance before him to their numbers while he deliberated his choice.

Hundreds of magazines circulated in America, ranging from fanzines and sports mags to the glossies. The glossies provided the ideal of style and wealth, those things and manner of living which are most to be yearned for, the ultimates in choice. Their pages were thick and stiffly shiny, you could cut your finger on the edge. Illustrations too were sharp in high definition, executed with bold colours in Art Deco design. The images they showed were of cars and planes and transatlantic liners, of grand hotels and racehorses and fair women, the appurtenances of careless wealth. Their message was aspirational: the pictures sold freedom-to-be, mastery of a fashionable milieu, familiarity with the capitals of Europe, a cosmopolitan self-assurance. The people in the ads were constantly on the move. These handsome men and sleek flat-breasted women in short straight dresses and cloche hats which looked like flying helmets were always going or arriving somewhere, and always accompanied by a large amount of matched luggage, skis, golf clubs and tennis racquets, which they left others to deal with.

Transatlantic liners were still the most fashionable method of travel to Europe. The five-and-a-half-day crossing could be enjoyed in considerable luxury and the modish company of the best people. Airships too now plied the crossing, providing novelty in ultra-modern comfort together with first-class food and wine. Aeroplanes were the most up-to-the-minute form of travel, ultra chic but only for the young and bold, for they were uncomfortable, unreliable and often dangerous. The first daily scheduled commercial air service, London–Paris, had started up in 1919, but not until 1927 (the date we've now reached in this book) did the US see its first passenger air service. At first the aircraft (the word 'airliner' had not yet been coined) that flew these routes were First World War bombers adapted to carry five to eight passengers well wrapped up for the trip. But all of these journeys were short-hop flights. Liners and airships monopolised the Europe–US route, no aeroplane had yet flown a non-stop transatlantic crossing. In the winter of 1926/7 Raymond Orteig, a millionaire New Yorker, offered a prize of $25,000 to the first man to fly New York–Paris.

Richard Byrd determined to go for it.

Undoubtedly it must be gratifying to become a national idol, to have plazas, schools and sons named after you and medals struck in your image, but the modern hero has a finite shelf-life. *What to do for your next trick?* He or she has achieved stardom, become a performer in their own soap opera. But a soap opera requires new episodes to endure.

Fame also brings with it a *personal* problem, a problem so intimate that the celeb cannot, dare not, mention it to anyone for to do so is to admit that you are *not* cool, not cool at all but only a needy schmuck made of the same base clay as your fans. This shameful frailty that can be revealed to nobody is that you have contracted an addiction, for the heady rush of fame has established a need within you similar in effect to some drugs which create not just a pleasurable buzz but an absolute require-ment in the blood and nerves, for nothing, nothing else can come close to the rush that celebrity provides.

Byrd already had a sponsor lined up to back him in the race in the substantial shape of Rodman Wanamaker, owner of the so-named Manhattan department store and a fervent patriot who believed in the popular movement America First. Now Byrd asked Tony Fokker, America's leading aircraft designer, to build a plane for the transatlantic flight. Fokker's latest innovation was wing flaps, which he'd invented a year earlier – still in use today – which considerably lower an aircraft's take-off and landing speed, permitting shorter runways. This device so opened up the convenience of flight as a means of public transport that there were plans to build an inner city airport in lower Manhattan on top of a 150-storey super-skyscraper at Broadway and Church Street, whose rooftop area would be a landing field. It was around this date that Scott Fitzgerald wrote to his daughter Scottie tell-ing her she must overcome her neurotic fear of flying and learn to board an aeroplane as thoughtlessly as she stepped on a bus.

It was Fokker who had constructed the *Jo Ford* and Byrd now asked him to build a new version of the tri-motor, modified for the 3,600 mile attempt. He wanted bigger wings with extendable

flaps, larger fuel tanks, more powerful motors and an exterior
catwalk, so if one engine failed it could be repaired in flight
while the plane continued on the other two. A literally hair-
raising scene to visualise.

There were a dozen other competitors preparing aircraft for
the race. With $500,000 from Wanamaker, Byrd had a deeper
purse than any of them. Most intended to fly a single-engined
plane, but Byrd's big tri-motor was safer and more reliable. Not
very sporting of him, some commentators remarked, but Byrd
had his answer ready: he wasn't interested in the race, he was
doing this *to prove the viability of transatlantic passenger flight*.
This would be an achievement similar to Bleriot's first crossing
of the Channel in 1909, which created the financial and technical climate for the industrial development of aviation. Bleriot's
crossing had shown air transit between countries to be feasible;
his own would demonstrate that a regular intercontinental
passenger service US–Europe was now a practicable reality.

In April 1927 the plane was ready for its first aerial test. Fokker
was at the controls, Byrd and Bennett in the pilot's cabin with
him. In flight the aircraft behaved correctly, but when Fokker cut
back the power to its 60 mph landing speed the plane revealed
itself dangerously nose-heavy; it would not glide. On coming in
to land the aeroplane descended at a steep angle, slammed into
the ground and cartwheeled, coming to rest upside down. Fokker
was thrown clear, unhurt. Byrd's right arm was broken (he set it
himself in the ambulance on the way to hospital), but Bennett's
leg was smashed and he was in a bad way. He was rushed into
intensive care but for ten days his condition remained so serious
it was uncertain whether he would pull through.

On 28 June Bernt Balchen was waiting somewhat disconsolately by the hangar at Roosevelt Field, smoking a cigarette. Byrd's plane had been repaired and stood inside fuelled-up and ready to go, but the prospect of the transatlantic flight was not exhilarating. Four of the contestants in the race to Paris had crashed and died in their attempts, but more crucially the Orteig Prize had already been won by Charles A. Lindbergh in the *Spirit of St Louis.*

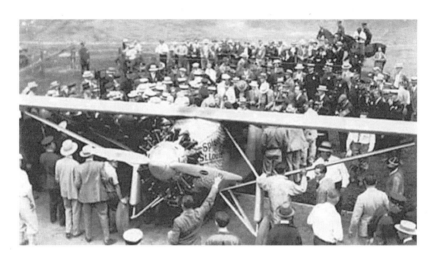

News of Lindbergh's win (after a flight of 33 hours 39 minutes at an average speed of 107 mph, in a plane with one engine, no radio, no map, no parachute, no life-raft, two pints of water and five sandwiches) had reached Roosevelt Field with particularly bad timing, for at that instant Byrd's Fokker was being christened *America* at a ceremony attended by the French ambassador, the media and 2,000 specially invited guests from government, banking, big business, science and aeronautics. This was a fully orchestrated promotional event and for the news to come through just now must have been a shattering blow for Byrd – moreover one he had to endure in full view of the public – but he handled it well, turning the occasion into a party to celebrate Lindbergh's victory. He had already done what he could to distance himself from the race, deliberately holding back from registering as an official contestant, but now clearly something more was required – and fast. Even while he was toasting Lindbergh's win, the highly effective press office he and Wanamaker had set up in the hangar was preparing a release announcing that the *America*'s hop to France was merely a test of the aircraft's long-range capacity. Byrd's next flight would be infinitely more spectacular and hazardous – he intended to fly the aeroplane to the South Pole.

But Balchen's dejection this morning came from a more personal cause than the above reasons. He was not included on the *America*'s transatlantic flight to Paris as Wanamaker saw the crossing as a patriotic statement: *America First*. He wanted an all-American crew on the plane. Balchen was not yet a US citizen; though he'd filed an application, his nationalisation had not been processed.

While Balchen was brooding on the injustice of the world, he saw a car pull up in front of the aircraft hangar. The driver sprang out to open the passenger door. An arm passed over two crutches and after a long moment a man slowly, awkwardly negotiated his way out. Watching from the corner of the building, Balchen recognised Bennett. His face looked dirty grey in colour and he was painfully thin. Swaying on his crutches, he threw Balchen a wave then hobbled into the open hangar to join Byrd and Wanamaker's publicist in the press corner.

Balchen saw the three men talking earnestly for several minutes, then Bennett detached himself from the group and tottered over to where he stood. He put his hand out to shake and Balchen was saddened by how weak his grip was. But Bennett was grinning. He said, 'It's OK Bernt, it's all set. You're on the crew.'

At 5.20 a.m. next morning the *America* took off with Byrd, Balchen and two other pilots on board. The only plane in the race equipped with radio, this was out of action for much of the flight after one of the pilots trod on the wiring. Thirty-six hours later they sighted the coast of France and followed the course of the Seine to Paris, but Le Bourget airfield was invisible in the rain. They returned to the coast. The weather was dreadful, it was getting dark and their fuel tanks were almost empty. Balchen was at the controls, he had greater experience of foul weather flying than the other pilots. With great skill he crash-landed the plane in shallow water off Caen. No one was injured and the next day, assisted by the local villagers, who stole bits of it as souvenirs, they dismantled the aircraft and carried it to safety up the foreshore at a spot which seventeen years later would become known to all America as Omaha Beach, one of the sites of the D-Day landings.

Despite the failure of the *America* to land in Paris and Lindbergh winning the race, which might have been expected to scoop the publicity, Byrd, Balchen and the two American pilots were received rapturously in the city when they arrived by train the next afternoon.

Balchen who had made the flight wearing a plaid lumberjack shirt and oil-soaked trousers, had to have a suit made for him overnight with 'coat and pants in the latest French style. The clerk wants to sell me a derby even; but I draw the line at that.' He describes the scene he stepped into:

> Never have I seen anything like the wild hysteria of Paris ... the streets were blocked with crowds, and they swarmed over the car and broke the windows and almost tipped it over. The mob pushed us down the avenue shouting '*Vivent les Americans! Vive Byrd!*' Women threw their arms around us and kissed us until our faces were daubed with red lipstick...

He found himself projected into a world he'd never encountered before, hardly had imagined to exist. He was introduced to the Prince of Wales; he met the venerable and shrunken Louis Bleriot, who had opened a new epoch of aviation with his historic cross-Channel flight; he met the equally shrunken Marechal Foch, encased in tight uniform, whose elfin chest was so medallioned it looked as though he was covered in shiny scales.

Afterwards, while sailing back to the States aboard the *Leviathan*, Balchen spent much of the voyage with Byrd, discussing his plan to fly to the South Pole. He and Floyd Bennett were to be the pilots. Arriving in New York they were accorded the same wild welcome as in Paris, plus a ticker-tape parade. In Washington (where Byrd was awarded the Navy Distinguished Flying Cross) Balchen was received by the President of the United States. For Balchen in his sharp new suit all was for the best in this the best of all possible worlds – of which he was about to become a citizen.

In August he packed an old rucksack and sailed on the *Stavangerfjord* to visit his mother in Norway. As the vessel steamed into Bergen he heard the sound of aircraft. A formation of single-engined Navy planes zoomed overhead, buzzing the ship in salute. In astonishment he recognised the wing numbers, it was his old squadron come to greet him. He felt something like love rise up within him and had to swallow hard to hold back tears. Over dinner in the Officer's Club he was reunited with his cousin Lief Dietrichson (pilot of Ellsworth's plane on the 1925 flight) and Omdal (mechanic on that same plane, also on the *Norge*) and Riiser-Larsen. 'How did you find the girls in Paris?' one asked him. 'Easy,' he told them, 'They were waiting.'

In Oslo Balchen found a suite booked for him at the Grand Hotel, and a messenger in the uniform of the Royal Guards summoning him to the Palace. 'You have carried the flag of our country far,' the King told him.

He motions me to be seated and for an hour and a half he questions me with shrewd insight about flying and the future of aviation, what it will mean some day to Norway ... He is particularly interested to hear of Byrd's proposed Antarctic flight, and as I rise to leave he says, 'We are proud that the American expedition is coming to Roald Amundsen for counsel. To honor him is to honor all Norway.'

The following afternoon Balchen and Omdal made a visit to the veteran, now-retired explorer. For Balchen this is a significant but also an *awkward* moment. Amundsen was his childhood hero and role model, the man who'd given him the opportunity to transform his life by picking him for the *Norge* expedition; Amundsen is a father figure to him. The two callers crossed to Bundefjord by ferry and saw the old man waiting for them, standing on the jetty.

We walk slowly up the lawn to Captain Amundsen's house. He is still erect and vigorous. His living room is starkly furnished and the walls are bare ... He sits in his favourite leather chair and listens with only half-interest to my story of the Atlantic Air Derby, but his eyes brighten as I describe winter flying in the Canadian bush ... Now he begins to talk about the Antarctic, the bitter cold and violent storms there, how to survive on the ice barrier, how an air base might be established...

Amundsen was open-hearted and wholly generous in his advice on the South Pole flight. He knew the Antarctic, he'd learned it the hard way during thirty years and he gave the younger man the benefit of his great experience. He even indicated a suitable ship for the expedition (which Byrd later bought), offering to negotiate with the owners. That he should provide such help to Balchen is understandable, the young Norwegian had been a protégé since boyhood, but this was for the advantage of Richard Byrd, the man who had triumphed over him. Byrd had everything now, while Amundsen was bankrupt and deeper in debt than ever due to the disastrous deficit on the *Norge* expedition. But Amundsen had never complained or grumbled, never uttered one word questioning the validity of Byrd's polar victory. Instead, he gave. He invited his two visitors to stay the night. Balchen writes:

> That evening, after supper, Captain Amundsen has his own special nightcap, a brandy toddy in a tall glass, mahogany-coloured and consumed boiling-hot ... 'You are young, both young,' he says, sipping his toddy, 'And aviation today is for young people. Old men stay home and write their memoirs.' But I can see that he is ill content with retirement, and would like to be going with us. There is a caged restlessness in his eyes, a touch of bitterness that he must end his days in an easy chair by the fireplace. He would like to fight the Arctic ice once more, to die with his straw-filled mukluks on, in the north and the great white silence. We leave after breakfast, and he stands on the pier as the ferry pulls away. His lone figure dwindles from sight, but I can still see the great hawk-nose, the face carved in granite as timeless as time itself, the last Viking.

It is an elegiac tone Balchen adopts when writing of his visit to Amundsen but his emotions at that parting on the shore must have been both confused and guilty. Amundsen's melancholy reduced circumstances were directly due to the fact that he had not succeeded in being first to reach the North Pole. Yet how could Balchen console his old benefactor with what he suspected (or by now *knew*) to be the facts about Byrd's win? He was now a member of Byrd's team and on Byrd's payroll and the truth was something he could not *afford* to reveal. It must have been a poignant moment.

As soon as he got back to the States in October, Balchen went to visit Floyd Bennett, who was convalescing from his accident at home in Brooklyn. Balchen was dismayed to see how ill he looked. Byrd had put him in charge of organising the plane and its equipment for the South Pole expedition, and he filled in Balchen on all that had happened while he'd been away. The original plan had been to commission Tony Fokker to build a more powerful version of the *America* for the flight, but expedience – that obligatory element governing any expedition's plans – had resulted in another aircraft. Edsel and his father Henry J. had contributed substantial funds to the proposed expedition; they wanted Byrd to make the attempt in a tri-motor made by the Ford Motor Company. The advantage was that it came free, the downside that the new aircraft had barely been tested in operation; its flying characteristics and capability in Arctic conditions were unknown.

Two weeks later Balchen and Byrd took the train to Detroit to meet Edsel, and in March 1928 the two flew the Ford to Canada to test it on snow in sub-zero temperatures. Stopping at Winnipeg to refuel, they flew on to Le Pas in the far north. They landed into the middle of a rackety spectacular. The tiny frontier town was straining at the seams, for it was the site of a sensational gold strike. Prospectors, would-be prospectors, gamblers and adventurers had flooded into the place to stake a claim and throng the boardwalk and the bars – and following them had come a regiment of whores, raucous, gaudy and unsuitably clothed for winter. Saloons were rowdy with shouts and argument, wild laughter, piano music, stinking of whisky, spilled beer, sweat, cheap perfume and tobacco smoke. Raw gold, in the form of dust or nuggets, was the common currency of the town. Hotels, saloons, stores and the parlour of every hooker were equipped with scales. Here, in the bars, gambling joints and dance halls of this honky-tonk outpost throbbing in the hectic fever of a gold rush, Balchen and Bennett relaxed awhile, as best friends may in such untrammelled circumstances if they happen to be male. It is fitting they should share this furlough, for it would prove to be their last.

Then they took off for Reindeer Lake, deep in the snow-covered Canadian bush. There they flew cold weather performance tests – the results of which were disturbing. Then they piloted the plane back to Detroit, discussed the further work necessary, and caught the train to New York. When they drew into Grand Central Station they saw the newspaper headlines: BREMEN FLIERS DOWN IN LABRADOR.

The *Bremen*, a Junkers monoplane belonging to Baron von Huenefeld, had been trying to cross the Atlantic from Europe to America, which meant flying into the prevailing wind. Eight aircraft and their crews recently had gone down in the attempt. Now the Junkers was reported to have crash-landed on Greenly Island in the Gulf of St Lawrence. The crew were unhurt but their plane damaged and unable to take off without spare parts.

Aviators were few in number. Flying was a haphazard new profession and pilots saw themselves as a singular elect, the glory boys: a daring band of fairground, stunt and service flyers, well-heeled amateurs and penniless opportunists (with a handful of women among them, though two of these, the Hon. Elsie Mackay and Princess Löwenstein-Wertheim, had just died in their attempts on the east–west crossing). All were members of a de facto club, a classless fraternity with its own language, rites, rules – and a sporting tradition of camaraderie.

A Canadian bush pilot was the first to respond and go to the aid of the downed *Bremen* and its crew. Flying in to Greenly Island with a doctor in his two-seater ski plane, he left his passenger at the crash site and took off with one of *Bremen*'s pilots for Murray Bay. Plane crashes made good copy. A wreck, stranded flyers, rescue attempts… these were the elements of a front-page story and the editor of the New York *World* put his star reporter Charles J. V. Murphy on the job. To hype the story-value he asked the famous Commander Byrd to lend his new state-of-the-art aeroplane for the rescue flight. Despite his anxiety for the aircraft, which was precious to him, he agreed, asking Bennett and Balchen to fly the mission. Neither was in good shape; Bennett was in bed with flu and Balchen thought he was coming down with the same infection, but they flew at once in a Bellanca to Detroit with a replacement propeller and ski undercarriage for the damaged *Bremen*. Edsel Ford met them on arrival, and was so disturbed by how ill both were looking he ordered them directly into Ford Hospital.

Two days later they crawled out of bed into the cabin of Byrd's tri-motor and took off on the nine-hour flight to Murray Bay. Charles Murphy was with them. They had to climb to 10,000 feet to get above the weather. It was fiercely cold, and there was something wrong with the cabin's heater. Balchen at the controls became increasingly worried about Bennett who was slumped against the side of the cockpit, feverish and coughing continuously. He was running a temperature himself and so weak he could hardly hold the wheel steady in the turbulence they encountered. They were a fine pair to be going to anyone's rescue, he thought. By the time they reached Murray Bay Bennett was in a state of collapse. He was carried to a nearby farm and someone went to find a doctor. Next morning, before taking off with Murphy and a Junkers mechanic for the crash site, Balchen went to see Bennett. He writes:

> His face is the colour of the pillow, but there are blazing red spots on his cheeks. He does not open his eyes, but he runs his tongue over his dry lips and murmurs, 'Have a good trip.'
>
> 'I'll see you when I get back, Floyd.' There is a trace of a wry grin at the corners of his mouth. 'That depends how the sock blows.' His eyelids lift a little. 'One thing I want you to promise me, Bernt. No matter what happens, you fly to the South Pole with Byrd.'
>
> One year later I keep that promise…

But for now he flew to salvage the *Bremen*. Landing on the ice off Greenly Island, they located an Indian camp where they hired dog teams and drivers to reach the crashed aircraft. Then, having fitted the *Bremen* with a ski undercarriage and replaced the propeller, they could not get the motor to start. Recruiting every dog in the Indian camp, they harnessed the pack to the plane's tailskid and towed it across the ice to the Canadian mainland and an Eskimo village, where it could be recovered in summer. While they were arranging this, a dog team arrived bringing a message for Balchen. It read simply: 'Floyd Bennett died yesterday'.

Bennett was his closest friend, a buddy of the heart, and the news was wretched. Already sick and weary, Balchen was swamped by grief. This he records, and movingly, in the memoir he would write much later, but what he does *not* recount is the thought which must have trickled into his mind only moments after: that he was now the only man alive who knew the secret of Byrd's fraud. With such knowledge, what forgiveness?

22.

RE-ENTER FOOL

We are aboard the airship *Italia*, approaching Kings Bay.
Umberto Nobile struts back into the scene in full costume, overdressed for the environment but it is his nature to be theatrical. In the belted tunic of an Italian general, decorated with gold buttons, braid and bling, he looks as if he has stepped out of a band-box, but the fur coat he wears over his uniform, which reaches to the calf of his highly-polished jackboots, is more than sufficient to keep out the cold. Nor does its sumptuous bulk much impede him in his executive duties as he gathers up Tintina from her basket and moves into position at the forward observation window of the *Italia* to take charge of the descent at Kings Bay after a 3,300 mile flight from Milan.

Safely stowed in the airship's command cabin is an oak crucifix presented to him by His Holiness the Pope at the start of this voyage. The cross has been hollowed out to contain a document written in Latin script. The words are also inscribed on Nobile's heart: *This emblem has been entrusted by Pope Pius XI to Umberto Nobile, to be dropped over the Pole; thus to consecrate the summit of the world.*

So sanctified, Nobile is leading his own expedition to the Pole – and further. His life has been transformed since his intercontinental flight with Amundsen and Ellsworth. Unsuccessful and acrimonious though that flight proved, it had not been perceived so in Italy and by Italians in America. Following his triumphant entry into Seattle, Nobile made a speaking tour of Italian communities throughout the US. He was rapturously received everywhere and returned home to a national celebration in Rome. Mussolini delivered a speech of welcome in 'profound admiration', saying he had 'written an indelible page in the history of Italy'.

Nobile had come a long way from his humble beginnings. His own hard work had made him head of the Factory of Aeronautical Construction in Rome and the leading designer of airships in Italy. Today of course he was more than that, much more. He was famous, and he found the taste of fame's nectar wonderfully delicious; he felt he could achieve anything.

About his plan he writes: 'To tell the truth, so far as scientific observations were concerned the *Norge* expedition had not done much.' The hazardous nature of the flight 'in such a small airship had obliged us to concentrate our attention on the aeronautical problem at the expense of the purely scientific side'. But Nobile's new expedition would be the first scientific aerial exploration of the Arctic. 'I outlined to Mussolini, in an interview at which Balbo was also present, the programme of the expedition...' Balbo, was Italy's Minister for Air, who had vaunting ideas of his own for flying spectaculars and at this meeting he conceived a powerful dislike for Nobile which was both personal and professional. A reaction which Nobile in describing the encounter seems to have been blithely unaware of, but which would show its effects soon after. Nobile records only that Mussolini listened attentively, then said he recognised the scientific importance of the concept and that they would talk again the following week.

On that casual promise of Il Duce's – never fulfilled – Nobile obtained the official sponsorship of the Italian Geographical

Society. His hometown Naples was too poor to supply anything, but the rich city of Milan offered to raise a private subscription of 3½ million lire to cover the cost of the expedition. Its base ship, the *Città di Milano*, was provided by the Navy. The airship, designed by Nobile, was a sister of the *Norge*. Its crew would be all Italian, but of the three scientists making up the party one, Dr Behounek, was Czech and another, Dr Malgren, Swedish. Among all those aboard Malgren was the only man with experience of ice.

It was while coming into Kings Bay that Nobile received his first hint that everything was not exactly as he had hoped. Radioing to the *Città di Milano* that they were approaching and the ground crew should assemble on the snow to assist the landing, Captain Romagna informed him he could not provide Naval ratings to help until he'd received orders from Rome; it made a poor beginning, and relations with Romagna remained frosty. Nobile became aware that the chill was originating from Balbo. He'd asked for two seaplanes to be used for rescue work should it become necessary, now he learned the Air Minister had vetoed the request.

On 10 May the *Italia* started on her first Arctic mission, but almost immediately encountered bad weather and had to return to Kings Bay. On the 23rd the airship was ready to take off to fly to the Pole. Nobile writes: 'The engines were already running ... I gave the order, "Let go!" The men loosed the ropes ... And so the *Italia* left for the Pole on her last voyage of exploration, from which she was fated never to return...'

The route they flew at 1,800 feet was 'unknown to man', Nobile records, 'but with the wind astern increasing our speed, the journey to the Pole proceeded in joyous excitement.' At midnight on the 24th they were over the Pole. Circling above it, they held a solemn ceremony, dropping first the Italian flag then the Pope's crucifix attached to a tricolour sash. Zappi, one of the

Naval navigators, cried out, 'Long live Nobile!' The General adds, 'We were all moved, more than one of us had tears in his eyes.'

Then they set a course back to Spitsbergen, facing into a head-wind which reduced their speed to 40 mph. They flew low beneath a layer of fog which hid the sun, so were unable to fix their position. Fuel was low, ice coated the hull and formed on the propeller blades. The atmosphere on board had grown tense but Nobile says, 'The difficulties excited my energy; I did not feel tired but even more alert than usual.' He glanced at a photograph of his daughter fixed on the wall. 'Maria's lovely eyes looked back at me – they seemed to be misted with tears.'

Having designed the airship himself, he was keenly aware of the strain upon its frame and fabric from battling against the wind. He decided to reduce speed, but Dr Malgren the Swedish meteorologist came to him to say, 'It's dangerous to stop here. We must get out of this zone as quickly as possible.' Nobile at once ordered full speed. Earlier at the Pole, it was Malgren who had dissuaded him from continuing with the following wind to Alaska, insisting it was better to return to Spitsbergen. The young Swedish professor was a dominant personality, who throughout the flight had definitely influenced the decisions of its commander.

At 9.25 a.m. on 25 May – thirty hours after leaving the Pole – the *Italia* was flying nose-down at 750 feet when the elevator jammed. Nobile at once had the engines stopped but under its own momentum the craft continued to slant down toward the ice. Nobile was leaning out of the porthole dropping glass balls filled with crimson dye, timing their fall with a stopwatch, when he heard Cecioni, the chief technician, shout excitedly, 'We are heavy!'

The danger was grave and imminent, the stern of the airship was only feet above the ice. 'Stop the motors!' Nobile yelled, and pulled back into the cabin. Instinctively he grabbed the helm… but it was too late to steer. The command cabin smashed into the ice. There was a fearful noise, something struck him on the head. A weight fell on him, he felt himself crushed, he heard his bones breaking. He shut his eyes and thought, 'It's all over.'

When he opened his eyes Nobile found himself lying on the rough surface of the jumbled pack ice. He heard a dog barking. Fifty yards away the *Italia* was rising slowly, drifting away in the mist. One side of the command cabin was ripped away; from it trailed strips of fabric, ropes and wreckage. It was only then he felt his injuries. His right arm and leg were broken, his chest felt crushed. He tried to raise his head. All around him lay the pack ice, scattered with debris, a formless chaos of crags, ridges, fissures stretching far as he could see. A few yards away Malgren was sitting on the ice. Cecioni was lying a little further off, moaning in pain. Other figures were standing dazed, staring after the vanished airship. Beside Nobile was an enormous liquid crimson stain. Blood, he thought, then realised it was dye where a glass ball had shattered. Tintina was running around, barking with excitement. The pain in his chest made it hard to breathe, he knew that death was near. 'I was glad of this,' he writes. 'What hope was there? With no provisions, no tent, no wireless, no sledges – nothing but useless wreckage – we were lost, irremediably lost, in this terrible wilderness of ice. I turned towards the men, "Steady my lads! Keep your spirits up! Don't be cast down. Lift your thoughts to God!"' Suddenly he was seized by strong emotion. 'Something rose up from my soul… stronger than the thought of approaching death. And from my straining breast broke out, loud and impetuous, the cry: "Viva L'Italia!" My comrades cheered.'

Beside Nobile, Malgren was still sitting silent, holding his right arm. On his face was an expression of blank despair. Nobile said, 'Nothing to be done, my dear Malgren!'

The Swede turned his head to look at him, 'Nothing but die. My arm is broken.' He struggled to get up, his injured shoulder twisted him sideways. He said, 'General I thank you for the trip … I go under the water.'

Nobile stopped him. 'No Malgren! You have no right to do this. We will die when God has decided. We must wait.'

Malgren stared at him in surprise. For a moment he stood still, as if undecided. Then he sat down again.

❧

Six of the *Italia*'s crew had drifted off on the ruined airship. With Nobile on the ice were eight survivors and one man who was not. They found the body of the mechanic Pomella seated by the wreckage of the stern engine. Apart from Nobile, the group consisted of the scientists Malgren and Behounek; three Naval officers, Mariano, Zappi and Viglieri; the mechanics Cecioni and Trojani; and the wireless operator, Biagi. The unhurt men began to wander about the ice, which was littered with fallen debris. The came upon some cans of gasoline and about ninety kilos of supplies, mostly pemmican and chocolate. They found a sack containing a tent, a sleeping-bag and a blanket, which had been prepared for a possible landing at the Pole. It also contained a sextant, astronomical tables, a signal pistol and a revolver. Malgren asked to borrow it and for the second time that day Nobile stopped him killing himself.

The sleeping-bag was brought over to Nobile and he was eased into it while Tintina frisked around the men, wagging her tail and sniffing at everything. The tent was erected. The sleeping-bag was slit open and Cecioni, who weighed fifteen stone, laid beside the general. Then there was a shout from Biagi who was searching among the wreckage, 'The field-station is intact!' This was a portable radio transmitter/receiver which had been in the command cabin. For Nobile 'a ray of light pierced the darkness'.

Biagi switched on the set and tried to call the *Città di Milano*. There was no response. He kept on trying… and then the radio broke down. It was the final blow. Nine men and a dog crammed into the four-man tent. Around them spread a landscape as desolate and chill as the surface of the moon. The wind moaned, rhythmically flapping the canvas of the tent. Finally, from sheer exhaustion they fell asleep.

23

THE OLD CONTENDER MAKES A COMEBACK

The Grand Hotel – Oslo's most prestigious venue – exists in a time warp untouched by twentieth-century modernity, which anyway is not much evident in Norway at this period. Behind the ornate façade, its cavernous interior is decorated in the oppressive style of the Belle Epoque with potted palms and much dark-patterned upholstered furniture. The ballroom, which is also used for receptions and civic occasions, tonight is arranged with long tables and gilt chairs to accommodate a banquet. The elaborately moulded ceiling, crystal chandeliers and swagged velvet drapes lend an air of slightly faded grandeur and importance to whatever the event being staged there.

This particular evening is in honour of Hubert Wilkins, who has recently flown the Arctic rim on no money in a makeshift plane he largely cobbled together himself and frequently had to repair on route. Soon to be made a 'Sir' for his achievement, tonight he has been invited by the Norwegian Geographical Society. Two places down the table from him, Amundsen sits among the guests, straight-backed in wing collar and ancient evening suit, a glass of aquavit beside his plate. Food is a matter of indifference to him, he can eat or drink anything, what it consists of is immaterial; those with him in the Arctic noted he could drink tea poured straight from a boiling kettle. To dine out is unusual for him; invariably these days he eats alone at home in the house on Bundefjord which he has managed somehow to hang onto amid the ruin of his fortune. Still bankrupt, proud, oppressed by creditors, he lives a stern and frugal life, yet to attend this evening honouring another younger explorer is an obligation it would have been churlish to avoid.

The banquet has advanced through its several courses and is coming toward coffee and the inevitable speeches which will culminate this evening… when there occurs a slight disturbance, a divergence from the normal progress of the event. A servant enters the room bearing a telegram on a tray. He is seen to whisper something to the president at the head of the table, who opens and reads the message. By now the attention of the guests is upon him and when, a moment later, he stands up with the paper in his hand, conversation in the ballroom dies away to silence. The president reads out the news that the airship *Italia*, commanded by General Nobile, has gone down somewhere on the ice while returning from the Pole. The telegraph message is from the Norwegian government. It calls upon the country's veteran explorer, Roald Amundsen, to lead an attempt to rescue Nobile and his men.

It is a startling moment for Amundsen. Hearing the president's words, he sits in silence, showing no reaction or hint of what he is feeling. It is perhaps five seconds before he rises to respond, but in that short while an entire cinema of incident surely must have flickered through his mind. He knows all about Nobile's present vainglorious and idiotic expedition, knows the man's hysterical and indecisive nature, knows he is a bumptious ass unqualified to *lead* anything. He knows he is a fool and he has contempt for him. All this is so… yet Amundsen is a man who lives by a certain code and surely behind that impregnable façade his heart is racing. For here he has been sitting at a dull dinner, a disconsolate old warrior obliged to put away his sword – and suddenly he has received a call to arms. What he must do is clear to him. His seamed face is expressionless as a tribal mask as he rises to answer the challenge.

24.

RESUME ICE

The pack ice somewhere in the high Arctic on which Nobile and the eight other men are stranded is an uneven ridged and craggy terrain split into a vast mosaic by cracks and leads of water separating the floes, some of which are a square mile or more in size. In every direction the scene is all-white, dead. The surface looks like snow but is as hard as sandstone and almost imperceptibly in constant queasy motion. The ground the men stand on, sleep on, is infirm; it could split and give way beneath them at any moment.

Except for Malgren and Behounek, these are men of the south. Latins, they are used to noise and colour, warm blood, food and wine, children and the comfortable joys of married life. Now abruptly they have been cast into stark hell. Nothing they know, nothing they are trained in, has any application here, no one can *do* anything. Only Biagi, the radio operator, has any occupation. The rest can only freeze and starve and wait.

And pray, Nobile exhorted them. He was fervent in his belief that God would rescue them. Their second day on the ice Biagi succeeded in fixing the radio. Five minutes before each hour he transmitted a signal, *SOS ITALIA,* to the base ship, which was about 150 miles away. They received no reply, though on the wavelength they could hear the operator aboard the *Città di Milano* sending dozens of messages to family, friends and newspapers in Italy. On other frequencies they could listen to the world talking about the *Italia* disaster and the plight of the survivors, if survivors there were. They heard pundits speculating on their whereabouts. It was thought they were down in north-east Greenland ... in Franz Josef Land ... that the airship had crashed into a mountain in Siberia.

Every hour Biagi tapped out his distress call... and heard nothing in return. Periodically the *Città di Milano* would trans-mit the same routine message: *We imagine you are near the north coast of Spitsbergen between the 15th and 20th meridian east of Greenwich* [in fact they were on the 26th meridian, far from the area of search]. *Trust in us. We are organising help. We are listening out for you.* But the men on the ice knew it was not true, the radio aboard the base ship was continuously in use and no one was listening.

Nobile was in constant pain from his broken arm and leg and his busy tormented thoughts. The tent contained a huddle of humanity, its space largely taken up by Cecioni, who had to lie outstretched because of his broken leg. He was suffering greatly, groaning and crying out throughout each night. At times he seemed to be almost mad, says Nobile. 'Wide-eyed with terror, he would throw his arms around my neck and ask me if there were any hope. I tried to calm and encourage him.'

Out of the wreckage spilled from the *Italia* they had gath-ered 280 pounds of food. Enough to keep the group alive for forty-five days. They knew their position, the sun had come out long enough to take a fix on it. They were off the archipelago of Spitsbergen. During their third day on the ice, a look-out standing on a crag reported that he could see a shape in the distance: Foyn Island. It looked to be only ten miles away. They were drifting past it at a rate of a few miles each day.

Nobile overhead Mariano and Malgren discussing the possibility of walking there. Malgren indicated Nobile and Cecioni. 'With them?' he asked. Mariano nodded and he said, 'No! That's impossible!' Later that day Mariano, Zappi and Malgren came to Nobile with a revised plan. They, the fittest of the party, should try to reach the island before it was too late. One can imagine how Amundsen or Byrd would have dealt with such a proposal from a faction within his own expedition. But, instead of issuing a decisive order, Nobile suggested the whole party get together in the tent to discuss what they should do. The group was assembled, and Cecioni became so overwrought at the idea of being abandoned he began to cry like a child.

All nine men crammed into the tent and debated the plan at length. Should the three fittest go? Should they all try to reach the island, dragging the injured men on improvised sledges? Should the two casualties remain on the ice with Biagi and the radio while the rest went? Nothing was decided. They settled down for the night. Nobile, cuddling Tintina in the bag he shared with Cecioni, found it hard to get to sleep. The others were so eager to be off, he felt estranged from his men. They didn't even *look* the same, 'dirty, with beards already sprouting and fur caps on their heads'. Nothing in them recalled the elegant youths he had known in Rome.

The night was not dark, for this was 24-hour daylight, but somewhere in the course of it the sun broke through the clouds and Zappi extricated himself from the pile of bodies to go outside to take a fix on it so as to calculate their drift. He burst back into the tent at once saying in a loud awed whisper, 'There's a bear!'

Malgren – who'd by now established that his shoulder was not broken as he'd thought, and had recovered from his earlier despair – was the first to respond. 'Give me the pistol.' Taking it, he went outside, ordering them to stay quiet. They crept out the tent after him to watch. The polar bear stood seven or eight feet tall on the other side of the tent, looking at them with small black eyes. Notoriously ferocious animals, when they charge it is with the locomotive power of a train; it requires a large-calibre rifle and a well-aimed shot to stop them. Yet with a single shot from a revolver Malgren hit the bear in the heart and dropped him dead.

The drama was over in a moment. Lucky shot or not, the kill was immediate and the huge beast lay dead before them. By that act the party of castaways acquired 400 pounds of fresh meat – and Malgren became de facto leader of the tribe. There was no debate, his kingship was recognised at once. Something elementally symbolic had taken place and, without even being conscious of it, the group of young twentieth-century Italians had retrogressed in an instant to become a primeval tribe. Malgren informed Nobile that the fittest men would leave at once to try to reach the island. It was vital the party should be led by someone who knew the Arctic – and he was the only man who did. He, Zappi and Mariano would go to look for help, the rest remain.

While the three prepared for their journey Nobile and the others wrote letters to their wives and families for them to carry.

> The stuffy tent was suddenly filled with memories of our dear ones far away; in the silence that settled on us one heard the scratching of pencils on paper … Then I looked at Cecioni. The poor man had put down a few lines then been too upset to go on. I glanced at what he had written; it revealed all his despair, his anguish … 'No, it isn't certain we shall die here,' I said. 'You must write differently. Hand it over, I will write and you shall copy it out.'

That done, Nobile then scribbled seven pages to his own wife, including a few lines to Maria: 'You must keep Mummy from crying if I don't come back again...' The letters were given to those leaving. The three men said goodbye in an emotional fare-well, shouldered their bundles and started on their march.

At the official enquiry in Rome which followed these events ten months afterwards, importance was attached to the fact that, while in the tent, the Swedish scientist Behounek had entrusted letters to Malgren to take home, but *it appears that neither Zappi nor Mariano was aware that Malgren was carrying these on him.* In view of what will occur later between Malgren and the two Italians, the reader also may find the fact significant.

For twelve days Biagi continued to send out SOS calls but no one heard them. Yet the wireless was working perfectly. The six men remaining on the ice could hear the near-continuous transmissions from the *Città di Milano*, and by turning to national radio in Rome they could catch news reports on the disaster – which grew fewer as the days passed. At the start of June they listened to the President of the Italian Senate announce that they had sacrificed their lives for Italy in the name of science. They had been given up for dead.

The group passed all their time trying to stay warm in the crowded tent. They ate bear meat, which they cooked after a fashion on a gasoline fire. They talked a lot – of home, of the past, of the crash and the fate of their companions who had drifted off in the wrecked airship. All the Italians except for Nobile were sunk in gloom, particularly Trojani, who was so stunned by melancholy he could barely speak. Nobile tried to encourage them. 'I believed in prayer ... We can die quite tranquilly ... We have done our duty ... we have fulfilled the mission confided to us by the Pope, and Italy knows this. The Cross and our national flag have descended upon the Pole...' The group's response to this was less than wholehearted. Poor Cecioni was so anguished by the idea of abandonment that he spent his days sitting in the snow trying to build a sledge from the twisted scraps of metal fallen from the *Italia*. A hopeless task, which made him weep with frustration.

On Nobile's suggestion Biagi was now transmitting an SOS from 8–9 p.m, as well as just before each hour. He was a nervy irritable man and no one interrupted him at these times; he was left alone to continue at his thankless task. But on the evening of 6 June suddenly he shouted, 'They've heard us!' Nobile crawled over to read the message as he wrote it down: *The Soviet Embassy has informed the Italian Government that…*

By some quirk of the airwaves a Russian ham operator had picked up a faint fragment of morse from one of his transmissions. It took a while to convince the Russian authorities of the authenticity of what he'd heard, still longer to interpret the text: SOS FOYNCIRCA. Did it mean Franz Josef Land?

But next day the *Città di Milano* was in touch with them directly. The Court of Inquiry held later in Rome – having listened to the evidence but expediently pre-decided where blame for the disaster must fall – concluded that the base ship had been unable to hear them before because of interference from the Kings Bay transmitter, but the shameful truth was otherwise. They'd been too busy chatting with the world to maintain a radio watch. So gloomy before, the party on the ice became manic with anticipation. 'How splendid it was to see my men laughing again – dirty, grimy, ragged as they were!' They celebrated with a sumptuous meal. 'But it's not over yet,' Noble warned them.

It wasn't, though many efforts were in hand to reach them. The Russian ice-breaker *Krussin* was trying to smash a path through to them from the east; the *Hobby* (Amundsen's earlier base ship) was steaming through the broken ice with two small aeroplanes on deck; a Captain Maddalena was on his way from Italy with a flying boat; Amundsen was preparing to come to their rescue with a French amphibian…

Nobile drafted long messages of advice and requests for his party's needs. He had nothing else to do, and these became so detailed that Captain Romagna – not by nature the most sympathetic and caring of men – told him to shut up and conserve his batteries. In the rush of excitement at making contact with the world the Italians had dyed their tent scarlet to make it easier to spot – with the shot bear's blood, the press reported. For the first time they went to look for a level area where an aeroplane might land. They built a bonfire, kept the signal pistol to hand, and maintained a look-out, but no plane came. As the days passed, the men on the ice suffered the anguish of hope deferred…

25.

EXIT OLD STAGER

Outside the protection of Tromsö's harbour the sea is choppy, and the big Latham amphibian wallows in the waves as it taxis into position for take-off. Seated by the pilot at the front of the open cabin, Amundsen straps on his seatbelt...

Only days before in the ballroom of the Grand Hotel and the company of eminent guests he had received a message from his government appealing to him to go to the rescue of General Nobile. The request was flattering, for the world thought of Amundsen – if it thought at all – as a has-been. He'd answered the call, accepting the assignment. But no funds to pay for the attempt were immediately forthcoming; he'd had to beg what he needed on credit. To put together this rescue flight had proved a weary task, he'd paid a price in nerves and patience. There were men ready to accompany him on the mission – there were men who'd follow him to the end of the earth – but the prime requirement was a plane. He located several but inevitably came the question: 'Who is to pay for this?' The Norwegian government. 'Yes, but...' Once again he felt the humiliation which came from recognising that his own word was no longer good. He was tainted by bankruptcy, poverty and suspicion of fraud as he had been for years; in his one chance of breaking free to restore his fortune he'd been beaten to the goal by Byrd.

At length Amundsen obtained a plane. He'd extracted this Latham twin-engined seaplane from the French government, together with an equipe of three. The men were unknown to him, but when the plane arrived in Oslo he'd added Dietrichson to the crew (who had been with him and Ellsworth in 1925, and who was Bernt Balchen's cousin). Dietrichson is at the controls in the pilot's seat beside him now. The French airmen are still muttering in affront but Amundsen fixes them with a stare. *Do they know ice?*

The Latham pitches in the broken sea beyond the shelter of the harbour. As the plane turns across the wind waves slap against its floats and a splash of salty spray splatters the windscreen; the cross-breeze carries the whiff of aviation fuel from the port engine. At the controls Dietrichson lines up for take-off. He turns his head to check the interior of the aircraft, then glances at Amundsen whose craggy profile is etched against a background of moving cloud. Imperceptibly the old man nods and the pilot pushes the twin throttles to full power. Engine noise rises to a howl and the amphibian surges forward to bang across the crests, casting spray. It skims and lifts off, the banging ceases and becomes a persistent roar. At 500 feet the pilot banks the aircraft to take the course he has been given… and Amundsen leaves the stage for the last time.

His plane becomes tiny in the distance and is lost behind the scudding clouds. There is no glory in his departure, no one was there to see him off. Appropriately so, for he's always loathed publicity and distrusted the press, who once idolised him then turned when he fell from grace. Yet he has never complained; he's stayed faithful to his code, maintained his troth. Indeed, it is his code that has brought him to this point. He has nothing but contempt for Nobile and the man's vanity, which has caused his predicament. But Amundsen sees it as his duty to attempt to rescue him… and so meet his own end somewhere on that vast expanse of ice.

26.

EXIT FOOL PURSUED BY JEERS

From their improvised camp on the pack ice, Nobile and his party see planes searching for them during three days. They shoot off flares, they light the bonfire, but not until 20 June does one locate them. Appropriately it is the Italian, Captain Maddalena. He drops them food, clothes and radio batteries. Next day come two Italian flying boats, one of which drops more supplies. The other carries a movie newsman hanging from the window cranking his camera. On its final pass it swoops low; the pilot leans out the cockpit to give a theatrical wave and shout, 'Arrivederci!', then zooms away.

In fact it wasn't 'arrivederci' but 'goodbye', for Italy took no more effective part in the rescue. Later, Nobile was bitterly disappointed by the way Mussolini and his country washed their hands of him. But if Il Duce was associated with an undertaking it had to be successful. Failures did not exist. Mussolini denied Nobile; the *Italia* flight was not a Fascist venture and he became an unperson. Air Minister Balbo's reaction was more up-front. He received the news of Nobile's crash while in Spain finalising the details of his own spectacular flight along the Mediterranean coast from Rome, with sixty aircraft flying low, wing to wing in close formation to demonstrate Italy's air power. 'Serves him right!' he told the press.

On the ice, while waiting for a plane to come and lift them out, Nobile worked out the order in which his men would leave. At the top of the list he put Cecioni, last himself. On 24 June their rescuers came in sight, a seaplane accompanied by a Fokker fitted with skis. There was no open water available for the amphibian; it circled while the Fokker put down on the ice 150 yards from the tent. The pilot Lundborg got out, leaving the motor running. He was taken to Nobile, and said, 'General, I have come to fetch you all. You must come first!'

'Impossible,' Nobile replied, and pointed to Cecioni. 'Take him first.'

'No! I have orders to bring you first, because we need your instructions to start looking for the others,' Lundborg told him.

This is how Nobile described their exchange to the Commission of Inquiry. He says he took 'the others' to mean those carried away in the airship and understood the logic of wanting him to direct their rescue, but again he insisted Cecioni leave first. Lundborg became impatient; Cecioni was too heavy, he'd have to leave his co-pilot behind and that was impossible. 'Please hurry,' he urged. Nobile asked the rest what they thought. He says they all insisted he go first. 'I hesitated … Then I made up my mind … It needed far more courage to go than to stay.'

He allowed himself to be carried to the aircraft and flew off, clutching Tintina. An hour later he was in Spitsbergen. He did not realise the significance of his action, but he was made sharply aware of it next day when Captain Romagna came to his cabin on the *Città di Milano* and said, 'People might criticise you for coming first, General. It would be as well to give some explanation.' He was completely taken aback. He had already drafted a long wireless message to the Naval Secretary: 'I have come to take up my post of command…' Captain Romagna did not bother to transmit it. It was particularly unfortunate for Nobile that the men he had left behind could not be lifted out. On returning there, Lundborg's plane had crashed and somersaulted. Its pilot was unhurt and moved in with the others waiting for rescue in the red tent. After that the snow became too soft for a ski-plane to land. Responsibility for the men's rescue was delegated to the *Krassin*, still crunching its way toward them through the pack ice.

Meanwhile Nobile was left to himself, cuddling Tintina in his bunk aboard the base ship. His request to join the *Krassin* was refused and the cables he drafted were ignored. No one came to visit him or spoke to him. At a banquet in Rome Balbo raised his glass to the room and toasted the disappearance of the *Italia*, *while*, lying with a broken leg in his small cabin on the *Città di Milano*, Umberto Nobile was left alone to suffer what he describes as 'thirty-two interminable days of indescribable torment'.

There had been no news of the party which had left the red tent on 30 May to seek help, but on 10 July a search plane from the *Krassin* sighted three men only a few miles ahead of the spot the ship had reached. A couple of days later the vessel arrived at the location to find only Mariano and Zappi. There was no sign of Malgren, whom they claimed had died five weeks earlier.

Neither man left an account of that terrible five-week trek, which in all that time covered only about fourteen miles. The story has to be reconstructed from the evidence given at the Commission of Inquiry, which describes it as 'one of the most tragic episodes told in Polar history'. The report is striking because of the lack of clarity. The facts are few and can be succinctly summarised. The first day's march the party travelled only one or two miles. The second day was worse. By the end of it Malgren was trembling and hysterical, the others could not understand what he was saying. Over the next ten days his condition deteriorated further. They were wet and cold, had no tent, and possessed only one blanket which they shared. On the twelfth day Malgren threw himself down and said he could go no further. He asked his companions to cover his eyes with a jacket and hit him on the head with an axe.

In their testimony Mariano and Zappi state that they naturally refused. They say he gave them his compass to pass on to his mother, but turned down their suggestion to leave him any food, which would only prolong his suffering. The two Italians dug a shallow trench to protect him from the wind, put him in it, and camped one hundred yards away. Several hours later Malgren heaved himself above the level of his grave to shout that they must press on. He collapsed back into the trench so abruptly Zappi thought he must have committed 'some desperate act'. He did not go back to check.

The two Italians continued their journey. Three weeks after setting out they were still a half-mile from Foyn Island. They had seen several aircraft but had lost all idea of time in the endless daylight. They built an improvised shelter out of snow and settled down to wait for rescue or for death. Fifteen days later they were found by the *Krassin*. Mariano had to be carried aboard the ship on a stretcher and could not speak. His foot was badly frostbitten and had to be amputated; he died a few months later. But Zappi walked unassisted up the steep gangway. He was in a highly excited state and unable to stop talking, though he avoided all questions about Malgren. He said they had had no food for twelve days.

With the two aboard, the *Krassin* continued the few miles through the ice to rescue the five men still waiting at the red tent. No further search was made for the wreck of the *Italia*. The *Krassin* transported the survivors to Kings Bay where Nobile was struck by Zappi's overstrung state of mind and remarkable physical fitness. When asked to recommend him and Mariano for the Italian gold medal for valour, he politely refused.

The Commission of Inquiry which was convened in Rome that winter examined every aspect of the *Italia* expedition, from its inception to its dismal finale. Its report was published the following spring. A discrete section of this is devoted to the behaviour of Zappi and Mariano. The manner in which this is written is far from straightforward and its sense is veiled by high-minded phrasing such as 'The truth in this world has always cost something to those who spoke it', and 'The Polar desert produces effects of a kind inexplicable in other regions of the earth'. Its exculpatory tone can only be decoded through understanding that it was designed to answer allegations in the press that the Italian officers had eaten their companion Malgren.

The most damning evidence was that of the pilot of the plane which first sighted them, who had seen three men. Yet the Italians maintained that Malgren had died four weeks previously. Mariano explains this by saying he had laid out his trousers on the ground to dry and the pilot mistook their dark shape for a prostrate man. But might it have been Malgren's partly devoured body which the two then disposed of before the *Krassin* reached them? There are other inconsistencies. One of these lies in the Swede Behounek's letters to his fiancée and sister which Malgren was carrying. If Malgren later decided to die, would he not have passed them onto the others before he did so? And why did he not send a last note, even an oral message, to his mother?

The Inquiry's report is much more explicit in examining other phases of the expedition. In the planning, the organisation, the flight in the *Italia*, the crash and its aftermath, it becomes clear early in the document who was responsible. And the culmination to this unsatisfactory commander's failings was that he damned himself conclusively by becoming first to be rescued and deserting his men. Nobile protested that he flew out first in order to supervise rescue of those who had been swept away aboard the airship. In that case, he was asked, why had he not put himself first when he listed the order of rescue?

The Commission of Inquiry had been ordained by Mussolini. It had by now been made very clear to the world that the *Italia* expedition was not and never had been a Fascist venture, but the men who took part in it were members of Italy's armed forces, brave warriors of the State. Nothing must tarnish their valorous reputation. It took four months for the Commission to produce its report – and verdict. Its members – admirals, generals and senators – knew what was expected of them and valued their jobs; all its conclusions were unanimous. Bar one, every Italian who played a part in the expedition and its rescue was commended. Umberto Nobile took the blame for everything. For the crash, the disasters that followed, for the death of eight men, for abandoning his post as leader to save his own skin. The conclusion of the Commission was: 'This action by General Nobile [is] contrary to every tradition and law of military honour. He had no right to behave as he did.'

Nobile was crushed by the verdict. But he was allowed no propriety in his despair for it was followed by a coda which not only robbed it of all dignity but flags that strain of farce which may be detected throughout his history. Two days afterward the Italian papers ran a story saying that how he'd really broken his leg was by falling over while running with his doggie to be first to bag a seat on the rescue plane.

Nobile was stripped of his rank. Ostracised in Rome, he went into self-exile in Russia, a disgraced and broken man, accompanied by his family and Tintina.

21.

STAR TURN

On Wall Street as throughout the United States, in this summer of 1928 this is still the best of times and daily growing even better. The economy and stock market are unconstrained in their growth. Everyone is playing the market now and everyone is winning, everyone knows of someone who yesterday was nothing and now has moved to Florida a millionaire. People trade tips – in the barber's shop, at the shoeshine stand, in the elevator; groups of strangers swap tips in the subway. The country is united in a great democracy of prosperous optimism.

Meanwhile President Coolidge got through with work by lunchtime, then snoozed in his rocker on the porch of the White House. It was not that he did *nothing*. He listened to those who came to see him in the Oval Office in the course of the morning, seldom saying anything himself; he discussed that day's menus with the White House cook and carefully went over her expenditure. At the height of the Wall Street hysteria the Federal Reserve Board begged Coolidge to put on the brakes and tighten the money supply. Instead he issued a statement that the $4 billion (equivalent to $50 billion today) currently out in brokers' loans represented only 'a natural expansion of business in the security market'. The afternoon that officials from the Treasury Department came to him to demand immediate and drastic controls on the market coincided with his receiving the gift of a barrel of apples from a friend in his native Vermont. Coolidge received the delegates in icy silence, waved off their proposals...and went down to the White House basement to count the number of apples in the barrel. All the while he reigned over this orgy of profligacy taking place throughout the country – during which his Secretary of the Treasury, Andrew Mellon, legitimately and honestly made a personal profit of $3 billion on the market – he was diligently saving money from his presidential salary. In 1927 Coolidge looked certain to be re-elected the following year, yet inexplicably he chose to step down. He offered no reason, then or later. He dictated a ten-word message to the nation: 'I do not choose to run for President in 1928.' That was all, he was not a gabby man, but was it because he glimpsed a shadow of the catastrophe that lay ahead? No shadow was visible to the American people; Herbert Hoover came into office to inform them they could look forward to two chickens in every pot and two cars in every garage as no more than their rightful reasonable expectation. Wall Street responded. Shares rose... and rose... and the music went on playing.

Along with cinema production, building, retail manufacture and much else, 1928 was a boom year for aerial exploration. The period saw a sort of gold rush of the air in which the aviators were hardy prospectors traversing uncharted skies to stake their claim. As we already know, the Australian explorer Hubert Wilkins and his partner, a Canadian bush pilot (both of whom had entered the race for the North Pole in 1926 but wrecked their planes before the start), succeeded in hopping their way in a single-engined Lockheed Vega around the Arctic rim from Point Barrow to Spitsbergen. Two Italian officers, Captain Ferrarin and Major del Prete, set a record for a non-stop flight of 4,466 miles from Rome to Brazil. Kingsford-Smith piloted the *Southern Cross* 7,300 miles (with refuelling stops) California–Australia. And while Harold Gatty and Wiley Post were setting up their flight around the world, Amelia Earhart became the first woman to fly the Atlantic, in the tri-motor aircraft which Byrd had initially ordered from Tony Fokker for his attempt on the South Pole.

The question so often asked about Arctic exploration, 'What is it *for*?', can be simply answered at this period. There was hard cash in it as well as celebrity. Newspaper rights, picture, magazine and film rights, together with product endorsements ('as used by Commander Byrd on his flight to the North Pole') represented big money in a new age of mass media and consumerism. Of course none of these aerial explorers could openly *admit* to money as a reason for their pursuit. And, though they might claim patriotism and national prestige as a motive, nor could they confess to a desire for personal glory and column inches. *New lands* was the high-minded explanation most Arctic flyers gave for what they were doing, the discovery of unknown territory they might claim for their country, together with the mineral wealth which lay beneath its surface.

The largest area of unknown land in the world existed in the Antarctic. Sections of its coastline had been mapped – though who knew if it was land these hardy mariners marked in upon their charts, or huge cliffs of ice? Amundsen and Scott had trudged a path to the Pole, and in the past twenty years a handful of men had explored areas near the coast, but the vast interior was *terra incognita*: five million square miles of empty space.

Richard Byrd's mission to Antarctica to claim for America as large a slice of it as he could grab, and to fly to the South Pole to cap it, would be the largest and most expensive global expedition ever put together, before or since. It was made up of four ships, three aircraft, 150 men, ninety-four dogs, a pedigree bull, a herd of cows, two news film crews and an embedded correspondent from the *New York Times*. It carried 500 tons of basic supplies and was equipped to stay away for two to three years. Its scale and logistics were those of a small army – which indeed it was – with a mission to seize and occupy territory in the name of America.

Byrd and his planning team had their headquarters in the Biltmore Hotel in Manhattan, and it is indicative of his highly professional approach to every aspect of the venture that this accommodation had been obtained free in return for the PR value of his tenancy. Much else was obtained free; a task force of salesmen hit on every city in the US, hustling for endorsements, peddling logos and tie-ins, and touting for subscriptions. Very successfully, Byrd was selling a patriotic and uplifting concept for cash up front. Ironically, his training for polar exploration was more relevant than that of Amundsen and other rivals in the field. They had obtained their education trekking through blizzards and deep snow, hungry, freezing cold, often near to death. Byrd's had come from sitting behind a lobbyist's desk in Washington, playing the web of his connections. Unlike them, he could scarcely stay upright on a pair of skis, but he was an infinitely better publicist.

Ever since his return from Paris with Balchen, Byrd had devoted himself to the project with single-minded concentration. The magnet for attention and funding was himself, his charisma and what he represented. Celebrities are now so numerous and the commodity itself so debased in significance, it is hard to comprehend their emotional effect upon an uncynical public when stars were few. And Byrd was famous not just in the US, where a postage stamp had been issued to commemorate his polar flight, but throughout the world. His seed money came once again from his faithful patrons Edsel Ford and John D. Rockefeller Jnr, and his advisory committee incorporated the Secretaries of Commerce, Navy and War. The government, big business and the armed forces were behind him.

This exploratory crusade, equipped with the very latest in American technology and launched with the blessing of the President and a splurge of media hype, set off for the Antarctic in August–September 1928. Yet despite its heavyweight support and substantial funding, Byrd's business manager informed him when two of the expedition's ships were already at sea that there was a deficit of $300,000 in the accounts. Byrd longed to visit his family in Boston before leaving. Instead, he remained in the Biltmore, working the telephone in a final hunt for funds to plug the hole. His dedication pulled in over $100,000, but when he sailed in mid-October he still owed $184,000. The expedition was as well prepared as it could be. The unknowable factor now lay in nature. Success and failure are not nearly so far apart as most people think, he noted in his diary. Just one thing entirely outside human control can bring disaster, bankruptcy and ruin. The entire enterprise can turn upon a dime.

Byrd's main ship had been bought sight unseen on Amundsen's suggestion. The *City of New York* was a 46-year-old square-rigged sailing vessel, built to resist ice. The second ship he acquired was an 800-ton steel freighter, which he rechristened the *Eleanor Bolling* after his mother. He bought her despite advice that a metal-hulled vessel would be crushed if trapped by the ice. In addition to these he chartered two whaling ships – one of them the 17,000 – ton *Larsen*, whose flensing and butchery decks were each the size of a football field – to transport personnel, supplies and three aircraft to New Zealand.

The principal aeroplane, which would be used for the attempt on the South Pole, was the same tri-motor Ford Balchen and Bennett had flight-tested in Canada, but with more powerful motors. The *Larsen* also carried two further aircraft, a single-engined

Fokker and a folding-wing Fairchild, for use as back-up and in the scientific work the party planned in the Antarctic.

More than 1,500 men had applied to join the expedition. Byrd selected from them for stamina, particular competence, level-headed-ness and mental balance. In Antarctica they would be shut up together in close confinement for many months, much of that time in darkness. It was vital they should be compatible but, beyond this, they should share the same values and attitudes to life.

The *Larsen*, with Byrd and Bernt Balchen among the others on board, was the last of the flotilla's ships to arrive in New Zealand. The three aeroplanes, fuel, stores and livestock were unloaded onto the quay at Wellington, then it and the other whaling vessel steamed on toward their hunting grounds. The *City of New York* was loaded with stores, gasoline, coal, the *Fairchild*, ninety-four dogs and fifty-four men (plus crew). The rest of the party and further supplies followed in the *Bolling*.

Nine days out of New Zealand they met the first icebergs. On 10 December they reached the edge of the pack ice. At first sight it appeared static, a white frozen desert, but on looking longer it was seen to be moving, the vast expanse the size of a country was undulating very slowly in the swell of the ocean deep beneath. The dead world seemed to breathe. The air coming off it was immensely chill; the huskies on deck scented it, raised their muzzles, and began to howl together as a pack.

They reached the Barrier on Christmas night. Silent on deck, the explorers stared in awe at a vertical 300-foot precipice of ice rising sheer out of the sea ahead. The Barrier was the frontier of an uninhabited continent twice the size of Europe, and for days they cruised beneath its forbidding ramparts searching for a place to land. On 30 December they located an inlet off the Bay of Whales, close to where Amundsen had made his base sixteen years before, which provided a gradual ascent onto the plateau. Byrd and Balchen took two dog teams and drivers and went ashore. A few miles inland they found a level area exactly suitable for a base, which Byrd named Little America. The men aboard the *City* clambered ashore to stretch their legs, to be met by a crowd of penguins who rushed slithering down the slopes to greet them, pedalling along with their little wings, wholly unafraid and playful as frisky pets.

During the next six weeks teams hauled sledge-loads of materiel and supplies to Little America. There, Dr Lawrence Gould, second-in-command of the expedition, directed the construction of an extensive, carefully planned prefabricated town which they had brought with them.

After the *Bolling* arrived from New Zealand it took almost two months to complete unloading the two ships and haul their tons of cargo up the track to Little America. The days were shorter now and the temperature had dropped. Before the end of February the *Bolling* and *City* sailed for New Zealand, before they were trapped. On 17 April the sun appeared for the last time as a bright crescent flaring above the northern horizon, to set only minutes after it had risen. The forty men at Little America would not see it again until the end of August. They settled down to their troglodytic existence in the city beneath the snow.

The group of men inhabiting this subterranean township had worked immensely hard ever since their ships had reached New Zealand five months ago. Now there was little for most of them to do. Young, healthy, in the peak of physical condition, they were abruptly deprived of exercise. And closely confined. They lived like moles in warm humid burrows, scurrying at a crouch down long tunnels between the lairs. The entrenched correspondent Russell Owen describes how it was for them: 'We became critical, introspective, morbid, or indifferent ... With the sudden contraction of our orbits ... men stumbled over each other in weariness and vexation ... with the shaking down of our group came a conflict of divergent thoughts...'

The men passed their days playing cribbage, poker or chess, and popping corn over the stoves in their barracks. But idleness, boredom and close proximity worked their insidious effect upon the group, along with the cold and the dark. 'Our life at this time began to be disturbed by an atmosphere of uneasiness,' Owen writes. 'Things happened which should not have happened … Our situation was much that of people living in a community where free speech is denied, where mutterings and rumours and suspicion flourish.' There was gossip, and there were insults, arguments, ganging-up and fights. Byrd was the only man on the base who had his own room. This caused resentment in a society where privacy was non-existent. He saw it as necessary to his authority to remain somewhat remote. 'The Commander' was how the men referred to him.

Leadership has been a prized quality throughout recorded history until fairly recently, when it became tainted with political incorrectness, to be replaced in popular esteem by consensus of opinion. Leadership was taught in school until the middle of the last century in the same way as, slightly earlier, rhetoric had featured in the curriculum. The virtues of leadership had been drummed into young Byrd from an early age; he had studied it as a specific skill at Annapolis. What he had learned was Naval, which like military discipline is absolute. Every order must be obeyed, no order may be questioned. In times of war or crisis consensus of opinion is ineffective, a dictator is required. But in periods of idleness, boredom, inactivity and sexual frustration, absolute rule can give rise to tension.

The explorers Peary, Scott, Shackleton and Amundsen had all contended with the problem of managing a group of men through the long night of Arctic winter. Byrd's party of forty was much larger than any of theirs and – human nature being what it is – consequently formed factions. Boredom and morale were the principal problems, but there was a crucial difference in situation between earlier expeditions and this one – Byrd and his men had radio. One result was that he was daily reminded of problems with both his ships and supply system in New Zealand. The *Bolling* developed a leak; the *City* was hit by a hurricane; his business manager in New Zealand had a nervous breakdown and quit. Buried in the dark, there was little Byrd could do to help, and perhaps these anxieties fuelled a deeper fear which long had lain within him. He became withdrawn, at moments burst with irritation. A demon was troubling him in this long night and the effect was visible at times.

⁂

On 24 August the sun momentarily became visible above the northern horizon for the first time in months, though for several days before men had been climbing the radio masts at noon to catch a prior glimpse of it. Light and colour were restored briefly to the world, though a day lasted no longer than a few minutes. But to the forty men at Little America the sight signalled their enforced hibernation was at an end. They emerged blinking from their burrows into a landscape made of fire and ice, and set to dig out their equipment and prepare for the purpose for which they'd come: the flight to the South Pole.

The hangar for the Ford tri-motor had been constructed in a large pit in the centre of the camp. Now Balchen and his team of mechanics went to work on the motors. In a few days he had these tuned and was ready to take the Ford up on a test flight. He returned to report that it was handling perfectly. The aeroplane was operational and ready to go. Byrd had named it the *Floyd Bennett* after the dead pilot who had flown him on that famous flight to the North Pole, which had made his name.

On Thanksgiving Day the Ford stood ready to take off on the attempt. The movie news crew and cameramen were assembled for a last photo-call. Byrd, dressed in a fur-hooded anorak and polar bear trousers shook hands with his team leaders, saluted, then climbed into the plane. They took off at 15.29 hours. With Byrd and Balchen were Harold June as radio operator and Captain McKinley operating the mapping camera. The round-trip flight ahead of them was 1,600 miles. Its principal hazard lay in the Queen Maud mountains which rose to 16 or 17,000 feet. The Ford's operating ceiling theoretically was 11,000 feet, but she was carrying an unusually heavy load of fuel. There were two passes through the mountains, the Axel Heiberg Glacier and the Liv glacier. Both named by Amundsen when he'd come this way to the same destination in 1911. Balchen was sharply aware that, equipped with a thermos of coffee and sandwiches, they were flying at 100 mph over terrain where his childhood hero had struggled to gain a hard-won twenty-five miles a day, always cold and always hungry.

With Balchen at the controls, the Ford flew due south steadily at 1,500 feet. At 20.15 hours they spotted Dr Gould's support party, which had left Little America three weeks before, on the ice below. Dropping them a package of chocolates, cigarettes and letters, Balchen now opened the throttles wide and began to climb. Fifty miles away the peaks of the Queen Mauds rose above the horizon dead ahead. The mountains grew in size as they approached, a fortress wall flaring in seams of pale blue light reflected from its glaciers. At 21.15 hours they were at 8,000 feet and still climbing. Harold June poured the last jerrycan into the gas tank and dropped the empty container overboard. They were using 60 gallons an hour and had enough in reserve to continue.

The Liv Glacier, named by Amundsen for Nansen's daughter, led up in front of them in a series of frozen waterfalls flickering with pale blue fire in the sun. The rock walls rose sheer around them, they were entering a canyon with no space to turn around. The Ford was at 8,200 feet – which felt to Balchen its ceiling with its present load. He gestured to June, who was standing by to jettison weight. June reached for the gasoline dump valve but Byrd stopped him, pointing to the emergency food. June kicked one of the 150-pound sacks out of the hatch and Balchen felt the plane lift in his hands. June kicked out another sack and the Ford staggered a little higher. But not enough to clear the pass ahead. There was only one thing more for Balchen to try. He edged the labouring aircraft to the very side of the canyon, looking for a back eddy of air. The right wing was almost scraping the cliff. Suddenly the plane rocked in a blast of wind which heaved it up to sweep it over the crest with feet to spare.

Flying at its maximum altitude the Ford continued another 400 miles to their objective, reaching it at 01.14 hours. There Byrd sent a message, WE HAVE REACHED THE SOUTH POLE, to Little America, and dropped a flag weighted with a stone from Floyd Bennett's grave. Balchen turned the plane and headed back to base. He writes: 'I am glad to leave. Somehow our very purpose here seems insignificant, a symbol of man's vanity and intrusion on this eternal white world. The sound of our engines profanes the silence...'

On 10 January Larry Gould and his party returned to Little America from their eleven-week sledge journey to the Queen Maud mountains. On the way they had come across a small cairn of heaped stones, obviously man-made. It contained a can of kerosene and a box of matches in a waterproof seal. Also a note, pencilled in Norwegian. When Gould got back, he asked Balchen to translate it. The message read: *6–7 January 1912. Reached and determined the Pole on the 14th to the 16th of December 1911. Passed this place on the return, with provisions for 60 days, 2 sledges, 11*

dogs. Everybody well. It was signed 'Roald Amundsen'. He had been there, seen that, done that years before.

Byrd's message WE HAVE REACHED THE SOUTH POLE had been picked up by the *New York Times* radio station and broadcast live through loudspeakers to the cheering crowd gathered in Times Square. When the *City of New York* got back to her home port the following June it was to a tremendous welcome. The media was gathered in force on the pier amid a mass of people. As ever, Byrd did not disappoint his public. Although it was a baking hot summer day, he walked down the gangway wearing his fur anorak and polar bear trousers.

He came home to a very different America to the one that he had left. While he was away disaster had struck and the sun-kissed country he had sailed from twenty months before was now a desolate and despairing land of frightened people. The end had come, the climax to a decade of dazzling growth and gratified expectation. Automation – the machine harnessed to native know-how and inventiveness – had brought wealth to all. American business had discovered the secret of permanent prosperity. The stock market had gone up and up and up, most people believed it would go up for ever. On Inauguration Day, when President Hoover had assumed the White House in March the previous year, the Dow Jones leapt twenty points. In August it hit 380, at the start of September it stood a highest-ever of 381. Soon after there came a seismic rumble. The *Wall Street Journal* and the business columns steadied the populace, this dip was a correction not a trend. Nevertheless people had started to shed stock fast, on 22 October six million shares were sold.

Then on 24 October a fissure split wide in the solid ground where the nation stood. US Steel, which had been selling at

261¾, opened at 205½, crashed through 200, and dropped to 193½. General Electric, which had been above 400, opened at 315 and slid to 283. The unthinkable was happening. Shock, stunned disbelief... then the news flared down the electric pathways uniting the country and set off panic. Two days later thirteen million shares were sold, the ticker-tape was hours behind in recording the orders. On Wall Street people had begun to jump. On 29 October huge blocks of shares were being dumped in wholesale lots, and a record 16½ million shares were sold. The long bull market was dead, and American confidence and courage had died with it.

Byrd came ashore an admiral; he'd been promoted after his successful flight. Other honours followed fast. After a parade with band, drum majorettes and ticker-tape, there was a reception at City Hall, then the whole party embarked on a special train to Washington for a banquet given by the National Geographic Society. Among the distinguished guests were the President and Vice-President of the US, the speaker of the House of Representatives, most of the cabinet, thirty-one senators, sixty-two members of the House, thirty-five generals, thirty-six admirals and all the big-name sponsors of the expedition. Also Byrd's wife, who had just received a very special present from her husband: he had discovered and named Marie Byrd Land in her honour.

In the speech made by the President of the Society, Byrd was congratulated on 'the most comprehensive, dramatic and productive exploration of modern times'. The President of the US awarded him the National Geographic Society's Special Gold Medal of Honor. Next day President Hoover received all the members of the expedition at the White House. Filmed by a rank of bulky news cameras on wooden tripods, in a flickering strobe of magnesium flare, Byrd and four of his pilots were presented with the Navy Distinguished Flying Cross. But not Balchen; it was explained to him he could not receive the award as he was not a member of the armed forces.

Balchen was stung by the omission. With some reason, for the pilots of the crashed *Bremen* (two of them German nationals and one an Irishman) had all been given the medal. He was 'sick at heart', he records, and wondered what had promoted his exclusion – though he had a pretty good idea of it: his commander Admiral Byrd had been behaving increasingly oddly toward him of late. Balchen had noticed him staring at him coldly, he'd been abrupt and rude in conversation; Byrd's manner had become aggressive.

The expedition's welcome excluded Balchen, but it cannot be said he received *nothing* at that splendid occasion. As he was leaving the White House after being received by the President, a stranger stopped him outside the gate, asking if his name was Bernt Balchen. Sure, he replied, and was handed an envelope. Surprised, he tore it open. Inside was a subpoena from the immigration authorities. It informed him that he had broken his US residence in going to the South Pole; his citizenship papers were therefore void. The form was an official notification he was to be deported from America.

28

SUPPORTING PLAYER SEEKS LEAD ROLE

The image filling the screen is that of Balchen as, isolated by the event among the throng enjoying their White House welcome, he is handed the notification he is to be deported from America. The camera focuses on his stricken face… then the picture cuts to black.

The fade-in to the next scene is slow, two years have passed. This is the summer of 1931, and ice cubes rattle in the glass as Lincoln Ellsworth, stylishly dressed in a belted tweed suit and bow-tie, takes a long pull from his highball and looks down upon the Arctic Ocean 3,000 feet below from the de luxe comfort of the passenger saloon of the *Graf Zeppelin*.

Little has happened in his life since his flight with Amundsen and Umberto Nobile in the *Norge*, five years ago. Too little, in his own estimation, though one's sympathy for his plight is mitigated somewhat by the fact that on his father's death he came into a considerable fortune. As Ellsworth sips his whiskey in the saloon of the *Graf Zeppelin* his income from trusts and bonds alone amounts to $125,000 a year (equivalent to c.$2m today).

The *Norge* flight had resulted in disappointment and ruin for

Amundsen; Ellsworth had lost money and experienced equal disappointment. Perhaps greater, for Amundsen had already accomplished much in his life, but Ellsworth's dream of becoming a famous explorer had hardly been achieved. He smarted from America's failure to honour him, the man who had carried her flag on the first crossing of the Polar Sea. He'd told Amundsen it was 'rotten unappreciative'. He'd willingly accepted Amundsen's leadership, and with that renounced all publicity, on the flights he'd financed and made with him; but now Ellsworth was a novice no more, he'd served his polar apprenticeship and he wanted to be seen and *recognised* as an explorer.

He writes, 'Gradually the desire was building in me to go exploring once more to the ends of the earth … I felt I had dropped out of the world. I was restless, almost desperate for something to do…' He visited for the first time the medieval castle in Switzerland his father had bequeathed him, where every chair, every table, every bibelot was labelled with the price the old man had paid for it, together with the dollar equivalent. His son wandered through the innumerable rooms accompanied everywhere by the sound of the castle's 100 clocks striking the passing hours and quarters at more or less the same moment – a constant reminder of time running out.

Ellsworth had received a visitor that summer; Sir Hubert Wilkins came to stay. Wilkins had an Arctic project for which he was seeking funds: he wanted to go to the North Pole and make a crossing of the frozen Polar Sea by submarine *beneath the ice*. The scientific value of the voyage was negligible but he was a plausible fellow who knew a sucker when he saw one. Ellsworth writes, 'As he outlined the scheme to me, I grew enthusiastic for it … I consented to attach my name to the submarine expedition as scientific adviser…' He also put up $20,000.

Meanwhile, Hugo Eckener in Germany had been busy negotiating a deal to generate personal publicity and profit from the giant airship he had designed and commanded. In June, Hearst's syndicated newspapers flagged an upcoming first-time happening. The *Graf Zeppelin* and the *Nautilus* would meet up at the North Pole to exchange mail. Eckener had invested his own and his backers' money in a special issue of stamps commemorating the inauguration of a polar mail route, together with thousands of specially designed postcards and envelopes. He was in that predicament familiar to all explorers: debt. All explorers, that is, except Ellsworth. Eckener hit on him for $8,000, offering a place on the flight, the title of Arctic Expert on Navigation and the right to sell his own account of the event to the *National Geographic Magazine*. Ellsworth accepted.

The *Nautilus* sailed from Provincetown NJ in June, carrying 4,000 items of mail and Wilkins' party of scientists, pressmen and sponsors in a blaze of publicity, but almost immediately things began to go calamitously wrong. One after another every electrical and mechanical system on the ancient submersible ceased to work, and it was found that somewhere along the way the submarine's elevator had got knocked off, so it could not dive. The leaking hulk was towed back to Norway with its disgruntled passengers and scrapped.

Which left Hugo Eckener with a problem: The *Graf Zeppelin* was loaded with 600 tons of mail. Desperation kept him at the task and he fixed for the Russian ice-breaker *Malyghin* to pick up the mail aboard the disabled *Nautilus*. The *Malyghin* and *Graf Zeppelin* would meet to effect the transfer amid the polar ice. The Arctic postal service would be just a little late in delivery.

The above ludicrous chronicle explains why Ellsworth is sitting nattily dressed with drink in hand in the passenger saloon of the *Graf Zeppelin*, as he was at the start of this chapter. The airship is approaching its rendezvous with the ice-breaker and from the window he looks down upon an archipelago of barren islands sheathed in ice, scattered over a dark though sunlit sea. All are uninhabited except the last and most northerly. Standing off it is a ship, the *Malyghin*.

The *Zeppelin* descends slowly till her inflated bumper bags rest on the black water between the glittering ice floes. Ellsworth tips back the last of his drink and stands up. Going to the airship's hatch, he steps out onto the rubber pontoon supporting it. He fills his smoker's lungs with a deep breath of cold remembered oxygen and looks across the sea. A boat has left the *Malyghin* and is coming toward them, loaded with sacks of mail. A man stands in the stern, and as the boat approaches it strikes Ellsworth there is something familiar about him. The man waves in greeting, but, even when he steps onto the pontoon, Ellsworth has to look twice to recognise Umberto Nobile, whom he has not seen since 1926. He has changed dramatically in appearance, the whole cast to his face is altered; the *Italia* disaster and disgrace has carved him into a different man. Ellsworth puts out his hand to shake but Nobile pushes past it to embrace him, tears in his eyes. Yes he's well, he says, Tintina is still alive, his family is with him, he's living and working in Russia, but there is no time to chat. The boat collects the mail from the *Graf Zeppelin* and departs at once, but both men find the brief encounter moving. Ellsworth writes: 'As he left in the bobbing boat … waving goodbye as he stood unsteadily in the stern, the scene held an element of pathos I can never forget.'

The stories of Nobile and Ellsworth will continue to the end, but this is the last time the paths of the two men intersect.

From the milestone of his fiftieth birthday Lincoln Ellsworth looked back to review what he'd accomplished in the last half-century and found it deeply dispiriting. In the summer of 1932 he went to stay in Schloss Lenzburg to fulfil his statutory Swiss residence as its owner. There he met a young woman, Mary Louise Ulmer, who was making the Grand Tour – and married her. But marriage did not provide the answer to his restlessness.

By the 1930s all of the world was mapped and known – though not Antarctica, whose five million square miles of land or ice was still largely unexplored. And there at the bottom of the globe lay the one great geographical mystery remaining. Was Antarctica a continent, or did it consist of two separate islands? Whoever answered that question would fill in the last blank space to complete the map of the world. To Ellsworth the challenge was irresistible.

In the spring of 1932 the *New York Herald Tribune* announced the plans of the Ellsworth Trans-Antarctic Flight Expedition. 'Be careful whom you link up with,' Admiral Richard Byrd wrote to Ellsworth, reminding him of the problems caused by Nobile. But in this case he was referring to Balchen, who had transferred his services from him to Ellsworth. He's able to pay more than me, was how Byrd explained away the pilot's move, though there was more to it than that, much more.

In April of that year Ellsworth signed a contract to design and build an all-metal aircraft. The *Polar Star* would be a low-wing monoplane with a cruising range of 7,000 miles, far in excess of any aircraft then in existence. Bernt Balchen, together with his wife and baby, moved to live near the Northrup factory to oversee its construction. He was on a salary of $400 a month, plus a promised bonus of $15,000 on completion of a successful trans-Antarctic flight.

As business manager Ellsworth hired Sir Hubert Wilkins, who had clung to him like a limpet since the absurd collapse of his own expedition. Ellsworth, who was no stranger to disappointment himself, felt sorry for the man, sending him to Norway to buy a ship. Rechristened the *Wyatt Earp*, she still stank abominably of fish. When the *Polar Star* was ready, the plane was shipped to Norway. The fuselage was lowered into the vessel's hold and the little ship started on her 18,000-mile voyage to New Zealand with Balchen and Wilkins on board.

Ellsworth and his wife met the *Wyatt Earp* on arrival. Mary Louise chartered a small biplane and flew over the ship as it steamed out of the harbour. 'Mrs Ellsworth waved and waved again to her husband who stood on deck visibly moved and sad,' reported the *New York Times*. The couple had been married less than seven months and, in view of Ellsworth's plan, it was probable they would never see each other again.

29.

STRAIGHT MAN REBELS

In his small rank-smelling cabin aboard the *Wyatt Earp*, Balchen shares his cramped quarters with the *Polar Star*'s bulky state-of-the-art radio. It is his choice to do so, he wants to become thoroughly adept with it before they reach Antarctica.

Life has changed greatly for him since he was served with a deportation order three-and-a-half years before. He had not gone to Byrd for help with that devastating problem – indeed he suspects the problem *originated* with Byrd – but it was solved for him conclusively by Mayor La Guardia who called to say it was a 'goddam outrage', and he'd spoken to the President about the matter. Very soon after, a special bill was passed by Congress granting Balchen full US citizenship. He was cheered and delighted by the result. He writes that to become an American is 'bigger to me than any medal'. But the memory of that snub still rankles.

Among Balchen's first acts as a citizen of his new country was to marry, take a job as Tony Fokker's chief test pilot, and to father a son, Lillegut. From the Canary Islands, where the *Wyatt Earp* stopped to pick up water and stores on the way to New Zealand, he wrote his wife Bess a letter which was tender with love and longing. He missed her and Lillegut keenly but Ellsworth had made him an offer too good to turn down. A bonus of $15,000 for a successful trans-Antarctic flight was a lot of money, it would pay for their son's schooling, a home, car, and the trappings of the good life in America.

In the middle of December the *Wyatt Earp* reached the pack ice, and for the next three weeks butted and shoved her way through the floes to anchor in the Bay of Whales. Next morning Balchen and Chris Braathen, the Norwegian flight mechanic, strapped on skis and went to look for Little America. No one had visited the place since Byrd had abandoned it four years before. They found the township completely buried beneath the snow, only the radio masts showed its location, together with the tail of the buried *Floyd Bennett*, sticking up above the surface. Balchen scooped away the snow covering the fuselage and lowered himself into the cockpit. Sitting in the pilot's seat, he set his hands on the frozen controls, remembering the flight with Byrd when he'd piloted the aeroplane to the South Pole. Something caught his eye, an object lying discarded on the cockpit floor. It was his own miniature slide-rule which he'd used previously to calculate the mileage and speed of the *Jo Ford* when he'd flown her around the States with Bennett after Byrd's triumphant flight to the North Pole. Balchen picked it up thoughtfully and slipped it into his pocket.

When the *Wyatt Earp* was moored securely to the edge of the thick ice covering the Bay of Whales the fuselage of the *Polar Star* was winched out of the hold and swung onto the ice. The following day a storm blew up. Big waves rolled in, smashing at the edge of the bay ice. Starting up the motor, Balchen taxied the plane a mile toward the shore to what looked to be a place of safety. At 4 a.m. next morning the seventeen men aboard the ship were woken by the rumbling as of an earthquake. Leaping from their bunks, all rushed on deck. They were met by a sight so contrary to natural law that for a moment it paralysed them. A half-mile away the level plain of ice was erupting into a moving hill. Jagged slabs of ice were punched up from below with such force they were leaping into the air. A noise such as none had heard before was coming from beneath the sea; it sounded like a giant orchestra banging upon discordant instruments. As they watched, the churning fault-line raced toward the *Polar Star*. The ice the plane stood on heaved up and split. The fuselage thudded down into the gap. Men piled into the ships' boats and rowed frantically through the grinding floes toward the plane. The *Wyatt Earp* manoeuvred close. The aircraft was attached to the derrick. All looked on in stricken silence as the plane was hauled up. It hung there with undercarriage smashed and one wing drooped down like a broken bird. Many of those watching were in tears.

Next day the *Wyatt Earp* sailed back to New Zealand with the dead carcass of the *Polar Star*.

Lincoln Ellsworth was a supremely unlucky man, but he was no quitter. Nine months later he tried again. This time his plan was different. The *Wyatt Earp* would transport the aircraft and expedition personnel not to Little America but to the Weddell Sea on the other side of the continent. From there he would attempt to fly to Little America over what might or might not prove to be the 900-mile channel of frozen water dividing Antarctica into two.

The expedition's base would be upon an island where there was an abandoned whaling station which could provide some shelter from the weather. Appropriately – as it turned out – the place was named Deception Island. They reached it on 14 October 1933 in a gale of driving sleet which continued for five days, while the ship heaved in the island's lee. At last the wind dropped. The fuselage and wings of the aircraft were unloaded and dragged up the snow-swept beach. It took Balchen ten days to assemble the plane. He decided to test the motor and pressed the starter switch. The propeller made a quarter turn, and stopped with a crack like a pistol shot. Lubricating oil had frozen solid in the cylinders and a connecting rod had snapped. There was no replacement.

'I am determined to carry on until I succeed or see there is no hope left', Ellsworth cabled the *New York Times*. A new rod was ordered by radio from Northrup, who flew it to Magalanes in southern Chile. The *Wyatt Earp* set off with Hubert Wilkins on the 1,800-mile round-trip to fetch it. Ellsworth, Balchen and three others remained, camping in the derelict whaling station. Snow and sleet beat against the wooden walls, wind howled through the broken planking. It was a particularly desolate situation.

The *Wyatt Earp* returned a month later with the necessary part. The aeroplane's motor was repaired. But the snow covering Deception Island had melted, there was no place for it to take off and the *Wyatt Earp* sailed under low cloud in sleet and hurricane winds to search for level ice. Three days later they reached Snow Hill Island. But it was impossible to fly, impossible even to get the plane onto the shore. The blizzards continued for a whole month. A settled gloom descended upon the men living aboard the *Wyatt Earp*. The constant grinding sound of the pack ice wore away their nerves.

Ellsworth trekked across the island, searching for the hut of the Swedish explorer Baron Nordenskjöld, who had been trapped here through two winters thirty years before. He found the place exactly as it had been abandoned. The mummified bodies of three sledge dogs lay outside the door, where they had been shot when the party fled. Clothing and equipment were scattered on the floor inside. A clock on the wall had stopped at three o'clock. On the table was a gramophone, tins of sardines and a chocolate cake. He tasted it and thought it delicious.

The storms continued for two weeks but the morning of 3 January was clear of cloud. Ellsworth said to Balchen, 'Let's make a try!' While he was preparing the aircraft Ellsworth despatched a cable to the *New York Times*: 'FLASH. Balchen and I took off at seven this evening, heading for the unknown. The great adventure so long awaited is at hand. The motor is breaking the silence that veils the earth's last great unknown…'

Climbing to 3,000 feet, Balchen set the course given him, but he was not a happy pilot. In his estimation, Ellsworth had become deranged by his ambition. He had wanted to launch the *Polar Star* by catapult from the deck of the *Wyatt Earp*; where they were going to land, when and if they returned, seemed not to bother him. Balchen told him bluntly it was a crazy idea.

The sleek silver aircraft flew at 200 miles per hour for Little America 900 miles away. In the cockpit Balchen held the wheel steady while, behind him, Ellsworth busied himself with the mapping camera. To reach that destination meant validation and genuine achievement for Ellsworth, $15,000 dollars for himself. Not only for himself, for his wife and son. It meant a home and security, the grubstake to a new life. Throughout the last dreary disappointing weeks, to think about his family had been his only comfort.

Beneath the aircraft the sun glittered on the broken pack ice of the Weddell Sea, which stretched ahead as far as the eye could reach – perhaps all the way to the other side of the conti-nent. But ahead Balchen saw something else as well… and so did Ellsworth. What Ellsworth observed – as he recorded later – was a squall with the glow of the sun shining through it. What Balchen saw was a solid wall of cloud blocking off the route ahead. Pressing the wheel forward, he went down to 500 feet to look for a way beneath it, and saw none. Suddenly they were through the wall and in the thick of it, the murk was all around them. He banked hard in a full turn with the mist shredding past the cockpit window… only after minutes coming out of the dark wall into the sunlight. But now they were flying in the opposite direction, headed back the way that they had come.

One hour and a quarter later Balchen circled the *Wyatt Earp* and brought the plane down onto the glacier on Snow Hill Island. He taxied over to where Wilkins and others from the ship were waiting at its edge, and cut the motor. Ellsworth climbed out of the cockpit without a word. White-faced and stiff with anger, he pushed his way through the group of men and strode down toward the shore. Balchen followed more slowly. 'What happened?' Wilkins asked.

'Ellsworth can commit suicide if he likes,' Balchen told him, *'But he can't take me with him.'*

30.

HERO'S SOLILOQUY

When Admiral Richard Byrd returned to the States after his flight with Balchen to the South Pole in 1929, he came home a double hero; he'd achieved *both* Poles, the ends of the earth. His media reception and public adulation was wraparound, his celebrity stellar. To many he personified the American dream in its noblest manifestation: the dauntless pioneer who has won through to make it big. The public idolised him.

The Navy detested him. At a time when the service was being wound down and many officers let go, he'd come back promoted admiral. Such was his national status, so close his intimacy with the politically powerful, the top brass feared that Byrd was going to *take over* the Navy. Their fears were misconceived. Byrd had chosen his destiny – Explorer. For months following his return from Antarctica he lived on the adrenalin of applause. In his lectures he was fluent and assured, modest yet heroic. And so clean-cut handsome, his lack of height undetectable along with the limp as he stood at the podium. He was what they would like to be in their secret selves and they felt close to him. He did lectures, interviews on radio and in magazines, accepted invitations to speak to learned institutions and to open schools. But the era – and with it mass media, which had made Byrd – had brought with it an appetite for the *new*. Byrd was very conscious that fame fades and needs to be renewed; the action hero at rest is no longer news. But the mood of his audience had changed, for another pressing matter had come to dominate men and women's minds; in more than one sense to distract them, for some had put a gun to their head while others threw themselves from high buildings. The Wall Street crash had blotted out the bright prosperity of the 1920s and the nation was deep in the Great Depression. In the headlong course of that previous decade the Good Life had not just been invented, not merely shown by magazines and movies to exist, but *achieved*. People's earlier ambition of a full dinner pail had been sumptuously exceeded... and now all of it had been snatched away. A change had taken place in people's lives, cataclysmic in its scale. Black cloud covered the sun. Men with slack expressionless faces stood in soup lines, families were evicted from their homes, old people grubbed for food in garbage cans.

The country's savings had been invested on Wall Street and people had been persuaded to borrow on their houses, their farms, their businesses to put onto the market. When it collapsed not just their savings but everything went. Now banks were failing, factories shut, dockyards closed. Thirty million people were living on charity, a family whose weekly earnings had been $35 were receiving $8. In Manhattan a third of the city's three million working population were unemployed. Society women were selling their fur coats in hotel lobbies. In Central Park a Third World slum of cardboard and tarpaper shacks had grown up, without drainage or electricity. Hooverville, it was called, and there were Hoovervilles in every major city, filled with ragged angry people looking for who to blame. Big business and capitalism were indicted, the men who had ruled the country were named 'malefactors of great wealth' and stood accused of killing the goose that had been laying golden eggs.

When in 1932 Byrd tried to raise funds for another expedition to Antarctica he came face to face with the reality of the Depression, as against a solid wall. But he already had seed money amounting to $150,000 from his loyal patrons Edsel Ford and John D. Rockefeller Jnr. The first use he made of this campaign chest was to hire a business manager, Victor Czegka, and set to work on a lode-bearing seam which had proved profitable before. Now, by mining it anew, Byrd and Czegka obtained ship and aeroplane fuel, clothes, food, technical equipment and free radio-telegraph communication for his projected venture. And then there was the media. A contract for syndication rights with the *New York Times* was easy, he'd provided good copy in the past. But now there was another major player in the game: commercial radio. To William S. Paley, owner of CBS, Byrd sold the idea of a national radio programme transmitted from Antarctica. General Foods agreed to sponsor it.

The expedition Byrd was planning was to be the biggest, best equipped, most ambitious ever mounted. The goods and money he'd obtained were not enough, to obtain the rest he appealed to the man and woman in the street. His new expedition had a comprehensive scientific programme: astronomical observation, cosmic ray investigation, geophysical and meteorological research. All of it incomprehensible to the public. Instead, the dream Byrd offered them could be understood by anyone. To ruined and restricted lives he proposed the idea of a glorious adventure – the search for an untold wealth of treasure buried at the furthest extremity of the world. He would explore and map the Pacific quadrant of Antarctica, a quarter of the entire continent. He proposed to claim and annex for America an area of land in excess of 1¼ million square miles – together with all the oil, silver, gold, diamonds and other riches which lay beneath its surface. *That* concept people did grasp. They were used to the movies, it was their sole escape into a better world, but this one was in full colour and a promise they could play their own small part in making it come true. As the *Wall Street Journal* had exhorted them when the market first began to fail, 'Don't part with your illusions: when they are gone you … have ceased to live.' In 1932–3 the average Joe could ill afford the $1, $2 or $5 he or she contributed to Byrd's expedition, but yet they did, for the gesture purchased a share in something fine which transcended the drab mundanity which composed their existence. Hope was a commodity grown rare and precious, in their desperate need people bought into it.

Byrd's expedition sailed on 25 September 1933 from Boston Navy yard. It travelled in two ships, which carried four aircraft on their long journey south. Byrd's principal plane, a Curtiss Condor, had its supercharged engines and a wingspan of 82 feet; the Pilgrim monoplane was lent by American Airways, the Fokker by General Motors. The Kellet Corporation loaned him an autogiro, their prototype helicopter. Also on board were two snowmobiles contributed by Edsel Ford, three snow tractors specially built by Andre Citroën (whom Byrd had cultivated since meeting him at the Paris shindigs which followed his trans-Antlantic flight), and from the Cleveland Tractor Company a massive vehicle resembling a tank, which could haul a 10-ton load. All of these represented the last word in automotive engineering, but the expedition's ships also carried reliable equipment from a pre-technological age: 150 Eskimo sledge dogs and four cows provisioned with tons of hay.

On the voyage to Antarctica the ships stopped at Tahiti and New Zealand, and it is testimony either to the glamour of Byrd's venture or the sheer desperation of the times that, on departing, the *Bear* found she was carrying two stowaways, while the *Jacob Ruppert* had acquired a further nine.

On 17 January the *Jacob Ruppert* moored in the Bay of Whales at the end of a voyage of 13,000 miles. On the way Byrd had been troubled by a disturbing thought that Little America might not be there when they arrived; the Barrier supporting the base might have split off and floated away with the buried township. But he received an encouraging report from Lincoln Ellsworth, who was already in Antarctica. As we know already, Balchen and Braathen (both of whom had been there with Byrd in 1929) had skied over to find Little America still in place and the two aeroplanes he'd left there apparently in good condition, raising the number in his squadron to six.

Soon as he came ashore at the Bay of Whales, Byrd set off with half a dozen men to inspect the place. The route was unrecognisable, obstructed by pressure ridges and huge jumbled blocks of ice. Little America was covered by an undulating plain of frozen snow, hard and smooth as glass. Only the three tall radio towers indicated its position. The tail of the *Floyd Bennett* projecting above the surface enabled them to calculate the location of the main buildings. With axes they hacked a hole through four feet of blue ice and broke through into the balloon station. On the table stood a coffee pot, a half-eaten lump of meat with a fork stuck in it, and a loaf of bread. Someone tried the wall switch and the lights came on. The party dispersed through the tunnels to explore the rest of the township. A little while later Byrd, standing in the mess hall, almost freaked out when the telephone rang. It was someone testing the line from the admin block. Everything was as they had left it five years before. In the kitchen a saucepan of whale and seal meat stood on the stove. They lit the range, cooked it and had lunch.

The *Bear* arrived at the end of January. Both ships were unloaded and during the weeks that followed 400 tons of equipment and supplies were dragged up Misery Trail to Little America. The snowmobiles broke down, both Citroën tractors caught fire, the sledge dogs proved an unruly nightmare. It was very very disagreeable work in the ever-shortening days as the season advanced toward winter.

At last the weary job of transporting stores from the shore to Little America was done. The four aircraft from the ships were flown up from the bay to join the two already there, and bedded down in the snow. The *Bear* and *Jacob Ruppert* departed through the thickening ice for New Zealand with their crews, and fifty-five men, a pack of savage dogs and a small herd of cows settled down, happily and less so, to the four-month winter night of Antarctica.

Fifty-five men, the reader will note, not fifty-six, the total number of the party. For the curious fact was that Admiral Richard Byrd, their leader, was now no longer with them.

A part of Byrd's scientific programme in the Antarctic involved setting up a meteorological station deep in the heart of the frozen continent to record weather conditions throughout the winter, here where temperatures were lower than anywhere else.

In the nineteenth century scientists believed the world's weather originated at the equator. By the early twentienth it was thought that air currents moved across the surface of the globe from North and South Poles to the equator, where they ascended and returned at much higher altitude to the Poles. Weather therefore *originated* at the Poles. Observers monitoring met. data at the centre of the Antarctic continent could forecast the coming weather throughout the entire southern hemisphere. That at least was the theory.

Byrd's plan was to set up a met. station far south of Little America in the form of a living module sunk for its own protection below the surface, where a team of three scientists would exist for a period of six to seven months, emerging at set intervals each day to read the range of instruments planted in the snow above their home. This scheme was confidential; apart from himself only two knew of it. The plan and its details are fully documented in the several accounts Byrd wrote later about his achievements, but nowhere does he mention *why* he kept this plan a secret. It is left to the reader and your author to speculate on his motivation, along with other questions relating to the weather station which are now imminent.

The only people who knew of the plan were Dr Poulter, second-in-command of the expedition, and the cabinet-maker in Boston who built the living module, then broke it down for shipment to Antarctica, but both had been sworn to secrecy.

The plan to set up Bolling Advance Weather Base was not revealed to those at Little America until shortly before winter night set in, when a party of men and dog teams, accompanying the big Cleἀrac and Citroën traἀors (representing 13 tons of machinery), started out on their journey to install the base. The living module they were carrying weighed 2 tons; the rest of their load was made up of supplies, tools and a complete range of instruments obtained from the US Weather Bureau. As with all Arἀic expeditions of the period – and most later ones – the mechanical transport proved useless, unable to withstand the extreme conditions. The snowmobiles packed in early, the Citroën traἀors were unreliable, the tank-sized Cleἀrac broke down conclusively. It was left to dogs and men to haul the necessarily reduced loads. The site was reached, the prefabricated module was assembled and sunk into its hole – but there was not enough food remaining to provision three men through the winter.

There was enough for two however... Byrd vetoed the idea. The reason he gives for doing so – which we should examine –

is that two men living together in such close confinement and discomfort, cut off from the rest of the world for months of darkness, risked going mad or killing each other. *Instead Byrd announced that he himself would crew the station alone throughout the winter.* That an officer trained at Annapolis in the rules, discipline and responsibilities of leadership should choose to abandon his fifty-five men and six valuable aircraft camped on a slab of ice which might at any moment snap from its parent body and float away with his entire army into the Polar Sea, in order that he might pursue a private whim, is something that struck people at the time and since as curious.

We can however trace the origin of Byrd's singular agenda, perhaps even make a guess at his reasoning. Four years earlier than these events, in 1930–31, the young English explorer Gino Watkins led an expedition to survey an air-route across the Greenland ice cap and inaugurate the first Europe–America passenger service. A metereological station was established on the ice cap deep in the country's interior. Bad weather prevented relieving the station and a single man, Courtauld, was left to winter there alone through five months of solitude (he had no radio), for the last six weeks sealed in beneath the ice, in the dark and unable to reach the surface. The first party sent out in spring to find him failed to do so, and returned to base with its leader a broken man. The second, led by Watkins, sledged 160 miles to discover the remains of a tattered Union Jack and six inches of ventilating tube poking above the snow with Courtauld entombed below – alive and, even more remarkably, still sane. The story of Courtauld's ordeal excited a great deal of attention in the press at the time. As Byrd well knew.[*]

At Bolling Advance Weather Base, the party completed the

---

[*] This is related in Jeremy Scott's *Dancing on Ice: A Stirring Tale of Adventure, Risk and Reckless Folly*, Old Street, 2008.

construction of the living module, setting up the met. instruments in the snow above. They unloaded the last of the stores from their sledges and carried them down into the cluttered interior. The job was finished. At midnight on 28 March they started on their return journey to Little America, leaving Byrd alone. He would not see another human being for 200 days.

Byrd's 'living module' was an oblong shack of insulated plywood containing a bunk and a table. A shelf supported the radio receiver and transmitter with its morse key. A wall studded with nails was hung with his clothes; below it a victrola stood on an upended packing case. In the corner was an oil stove, vented by a tin pipe. Outside the shack was a vestibule dug out of the snow, with two blind tunnels leading from it, which were used for stores, and to house the generator powering the radio. Egress from the shack was a trap-door in the roof, reached by a ladder.

Byrd writes that he looked forward with 'keen anticipation' to the winter night. He had plenty to do: sorting the stores, monitoring the instruments, going topside several times a day to read the thermometers and to observe the sky. Additionally he set himself another early task before he needed it, he began to dig an escape tunnel in case his hatch should become sealed like Courtauld's. Excavating one foot per day, together with isometrics, constituted his physical exercise. At 10 a.m. on alternate mornings he made radio contact with Little America, talking with Dr Poulter and Charles Murphy, the journalist attached to the expedition (who had flown with Balchen and Floyd Bennett to the rescue of the *Bremen*). These exchanges were stilted, for though Byrd could hear their voices in his headphones, he could reply only in Morse code.

Until late April the sun showed briefly above the horizon in 'days' whose length was measured in ever fewer minutes. When he climbed the ladder from his burrow to read the instruments outside, often the landscape was obscured by fog or storms but on the rare clear day he saw around him a vast sheet of ice, not flat but smoothed out in giant undulations, stretching as far as the eye could reach in every direction. The half-disc of the sun poked above the world's rim to cast a path of flame across the ice, aimed directly at him; he was dazzled by its light. But from the middle of May there were no more such moments of epiphany, the night clanged shut on him.

He had purpose and occupation: maintaining the met. instruments and their records kept him busy, along with the chore of preparing his food. In the evening he played the phonograph (Strauss, Mozart, light opera) or read (*Travels of Marco Polo, Life of Alexander,* Somerset Maugham). He climbed out to observe the sky and light shows of the aurora streaming colour across the night. He returned below to meditate on the cosmos and to write, he wrote a lot… His observation of the universe convinced him that it was ruled by order and a divine intelligence, and from that he extrapolated a design. Man is part of that design. The goal of the individual is a state of harmony with the whole. Cosmic laws govern nature but also the psychology of the individual. The concepts of right and wrong are fundamental to that law, God-given polarities. To follow right makes for harmony, to follow wrong leads to discord. Harmony is peace and freedom, but for Man – unlike Nature – it is not a natural condition; an individual must *fight* to achieve it and it must be *won* through struggle and determination.

Four years earlier Courtauld in his tent buried on the ice cap had similarly brooded on cosmic matters, though to a different conclusion. Both he and Byrd were as isolated from mankind and the human commonwealth as it is possible to be, but Byrd's separation was not absolute, for he had a radio. Three times per week for an hour, sometimes longer, he talked with Little America.

While engaged in one of these lengthy exchanges around the end of May, he heard the generator powering the radio stutter. Asking the operator at Little America to hold on, he went to investigate. The tunnel housing the machine was thick with fumes. He bent over it to examine the motor... and passed out cold. He came to sometime later, lying on the floor and aware there was something he must do. He crawled into the shack on hands and knees and over to the radio. He could not fumble the earphones over his head so reached for the morse key and shakily tapped out, 'See you Sunday'. He crept onto his bunk and lay there, feeling weak and ill. He realised he was suffering from carbon monoxide poisoning. He could still hear the stutter of the generator and knew that if he continued to lie there he would die. Rolling to the floor, he crawled to the tunnel, then lay flat to slither his way beneath the layer of fumes to the motor and shut it off. He crawled back to his bunk and passed out. When he awoke hours later he recognised that he was seriously ill. His heartbeat was erratic and his whole body prickled with shooting pains. Although he felt nauseous he knew that he must

239

eat, it was thirty-six hours since he'd had a meal. The stove was out and the shack was cold. Slowly, laboriously, he managed to light the fire and warm some milk mixed with sugar. He threw up at once, but later tried again and nibbled a biscuit. Faint and weak, he forced himself to scrawl a letter to his wife and instructions to his second-in-command. He believed that he was dying.

For a week he lay on his bunk in the unheated hut, forcing himself at times to light the stove and eat something. By a great effort of the will he resumed his radio schedule. His communications, tapped out with frozen fingers, were brief. He did not tell Little America he was sick. He lay inert in the cold, unable to read. He had no wish to listen to music, even if he'd had the energy to wind the phonograph. The pallid yellow light of the oil lamp cast a dull gleam across the squalid room. The endless night pressed down on him in his hole beneath the ice. In the silence he had nothing to do but think.

In solitude, cut off from the stimulation and distractions of normal life, the mind is obliged to brood upon its contents; the individual has no choice but to embark upon a journey into him or herself. Solitude and isolation has been the path chosen by hermits and mystics throughout history, which, accompanied by mental purification and physical mortification (fasting, discomfort, pain and degrading tasks) can lead to illumination. The goal of this journey – known as The Way – is to break through into another level of reality, a higher plane of consciousness, a knowledge of Truth.

Was this Byrd's purpose in choosing – perhaps from the very start *planning* – to remain alone at the weather station through the winter? The reasons he cites for doing so – that it was brought about by necessity, and that two men left together might go mad or kill each other – are unconvincing. Two men would have been *safer*, and also more reliable in recording the continuous met. readings, which was the purpose of the mission. No, it is evident Byrd *wanted* to stay there alone, and early notes in his journal suggest that his motive was indeed very similar to the mystic's high-toned quest to achieve a spiritual wisdom denied to most of us. And at some point – perhaps a considerable while before – he'd resolved that he would *pass on* this Truth to the world, he would write a book about his experience and the revelation it led to. Perhaps by then he'd already decided upon his title: *Alone*. The gist of the Truth Byrd was working towards has been indicated above. He'd confided these illuminations to his journal during the early months of his isolation while he was in good health and spirits, but since his accident with the generator this had not been the case. Now he is seriously ill and demoralised, cold, sick, poisoned and unable to keep down food. As noted earlier, he has nothing to do but think.

What are his thoughts? In his book *Alone*, published three years later, Byrd recounts his physical symptoms and his difficulties in feeding the stove, preparing food and making sporadic radio contact with Base. He worries about his wife and children, he is anxious about the safety and well-being of the men he is responsible for at Little America... but beyond that he is strikingly economical with the larger truth. Doubtless these anxieties recur often, but where else does his mind go in the long dark spaces of the polar night that lie between? Where indeed? The present reader and the author may speculate.

The inner voyage of the solitary mystic is well documented, and directed toward an exalted liberation, a union with God. Yet surely Byrd's journey was leading him to a very different destination and a place where he did not want to go?

He must have reflected on his childhood – we all do when alone – thought about his parents and his privileged upbringing, of Naval College and the accident that handicapped his career. Inevitably he meditated on the progress of his life – and there's the rub. It has been an epic voyage, beset with perils and with challenge. He has battled to overcome his physical disability, contended with opponents, with the Navy, with the elements. He has embarked on great adventures at the head of his band of men, carried the flag for America, claimed lands for his country, named territory and mountain ranges after his family and patrons. He's been honoured by his President and become the hero and inspiration to his nation. And all of it is based upon a fraud.

He has lived with the lie for nine years. His lectures, appearances, writing, his gratifying intimacy with the great and good, and busy activity organising new and larger expeditions have perhaps veiled the thought from the forefront of his mind, though it has always crouched there, a dormant tumour lodged deep within his brain. With time he has come almost to ignore it for nothing has occurred to remind him of its presence and no one questioned his achievement or his fame. The tumour was obscured by the public figure he had become. Now in his sickness, weakness, and the cold of the long night, the tumour declares itself and grows within him. There is nowhere else for his mind to travel and he is obliged to face it. His life, his distinguished career, his public persona rest upon a fraud.

And that fraud – forced upon him in mid-air by the realisation that, without it, he and his family were doomed to bankruptcy – was no one-off. It instigated a subsequent *career* of deception in which he has bilked not just his sponsors but the people of America. In the depth of the Depression, at the worst of times, the average Joe and his harried wife had gone without to send him a ten, a five, or a single dollar bill to buy into the American Dream, personified by himself. And he is a phony.

He'd swindled them, swindled everybody. The knowledge is inescapable. In the dim light of his icy lair Byrd must confront the truth, and no distraction is available, no solace and no confessor. Does he feel guilt? Shame? Who knows what rationalisations he may attempt on guilt and shame, but certainly he feels *fear*. Exposure – that is the terror. Exposure of his deception means ruin and disgrace, a shame spreading to his family and children, and to America. But exposure can only come from one who knows the secret. The man who *did* know it because he'd been there was Floyd Bennett. But before Bennett died had he passed it on? Byrd's mind narrows down inexorably on the object of his dread…

Byrd's memoir *Alone* provides an account of a man steadfastly enduring a horrible ordeal. The reader's reaction is respect and bewildered awe, for how would one have handled it oneself? But the text's principal interest lies in what its author chooses to omit. He is reticent on the subject of his own thoughts and feelings, so guarded it suggests concealment. Somewhere Byrd says, 'I was brought up to believe a gentleman does not give way to his feelings.' And most certainly he does not do so when reconstructing those thoughts and feelings for posterity a year later while seated in the comfort and security of his study at home in Boston.

In his book Byrd confesses to nothing of significance; except between the lines there is little personal information to be found there. But it so happens that we have access to the testimony of another solitary adventurer whose experience was very similar to Byrd's. The twin accounts he kept of it, the true and the false, have both survived and are available to us.

In 1968 the *Sunday Times* set up the Golden Globe race, a contest to sail around the world alone, non-stop. There were nine contestants, one of them an Englishman, Donald Crowhurst (thirty-six), married with a young family. Middle-class, he had been brought up in humiliatingly reduced circumstances, unable to complete his education. His hobby was the new science of electronics, in which he showed considerable flair. Alone in his workshop, he invented a radio direction-finding device, to be used on ships. He named it a Navicator (There is an odd parallel with Richard Byrd's early inventions in the same field.) This inspired Crowhurst to set up his own company manufacturing the instrument. This did not do well; sales were poor and soon his backer, Stanley Best, wanted his £1,000 loan back.

Crowhurst saw the Golden Globe race with its £5,000 prize as a solution to his problems, and an opportunity to validate his Navicator. He determined to enter for it, though he had no yacht, no funds and limited sailing experience. He induced his patron, Best, not just to roll over his loan but to cover the costs of building a 40-foot trimaran, though Best expected him to raise the funds to pay for the voyage from other investors. He stipulated that if Crowhurst failed to complete the voyage he must pay him back the cost of the boat, and insisted he obtain a second mortgage on his family home.

The yacht was built and launched. A BBC TV crew covered Crowhurst's departure a month later. He relished the media attention, speaking at length about the electronic wizardry controlling the computer-operated craft and his excellent chances of winning the race. At 3 p.m. next day he set out alone non-stop around the world, leaving behind him a wife, four children, a house encumbered with a double mortgage, and considerable debts. In this respect his situation closely resembled that of Richard Byrd when he took off to fly to the North Pole in the race of 1926. If he succeeded in his goal he would achieve fame, and fame would enable him to sell his Navicator worldwide, bring untold benefits and solve all his problems.

Things started to go wrong quickly on the voyage. The 'waterproof' hatches and twin hulls leaked, the self-steering gear broke down, the generator flooded. Yet his reported daily distances were good. The BBC had given him a tape-recorder and 16mm camera. The footage he shot pictures him fixing his position by the sun while the yacht surges on unaided, with its course and setting of its sails cybernetically controlled. The film shows the wires that run down the mast, run everywhere... all connecting to the sealed compartment which houses his state-of-the-art computer. His clipped-voice commentary modestly understates the dangers of the voyage, at moments achieving an exalted tone eerily similar to sections of *Alone*. 'I feel like somebody who's been given a tremendous opportunity to impart a message,' he confides, 'some profound observation that will save the world.'

In contrast to these lofty sentiments and stirring footage, Crowhurst's reality was dire. He was in a leaking ill-fitted boat in the middle of the Atlantic while all his competitors were ahead of him. Rather than accept failure, he decided to fake his circumnavigation. He started a second log book, while in the first he marked a series of false positions placing his yacht further and further on her swift course around the world. In January he reported that he was in the Indian ocean, but having trouble with the generator. Then his transmissions ceased for eleven weeks. This did not stop his PR agent in England from feeding the media with his adventures. *Crowhurst limps on after battering by giant wave* was the headline in the *Sunday Times*.

From mid-January to the end of March Crowhurst cruised an erratic course off the coast of South America. He'd given up on any attempt to circumnavigate the globe; he went the way the wind blew. Meanwhile, due to his agent's releases, he was getting increasing coverage in the media. Much attention was focused on his computer, he was slicing his way around the world at the cutting edge of his own prototypal technology in an ultra-modern epic.

All this while his yacht wallowed aimlessly off the coast of South America. In mid-April he was reported around the Horn on a course for England, now the favourite to win the race with its prize of £5,000 in cash.

Hoisting full sail, he raced for home. On 23 May he learned that his last remaining competitor in the race had sunk. If he made it back to Teignmouth he had won.

For Crowhurst the news was dazzling, but such triumph meant scrutiny of his log, not just by the race organisers but at the Institution of Navigation. And he knew it would not stand up. There were discrepancies, he could not get away with it. He cast off sail and began to coast. When he broke radio silence on 22 June, his agent informed him excitedly that he'd sold serial and syndication rights to Crowhurst's story. The BBC wanted to meet him with a flotilla of boats, helicopters, and two camera crews.

What could he do? His log book wouldn't pass. The glittering prize and answer to his life lay only a reach away. But there was no way he could carry it off. For Crowhurst, it must have meant the most debilitating apprehension, a plunge into hell... yet his mind transcended it. The voyage *had* a purpose, he realised. From the start the journey had been toward Truth, and he had reached Truth; he had uncovered the cosmic message he must pass on to the world. In the yacht's littered cabin, Crowhurst drew the (true) logbook to him, turned to a fresh page and wrote at the top: PHILOSOPHY. He wrote without stopping for thirty hours. He continued writing for the next eight days, his philosophic message extended to 25,000 words. On 1 July he came toward his conclusion:

> ... Now is revealed the true nature
> and purpose and power
> of the game my offence I am
> I am what I am and I
> see the nature of my offence...
> It is finished
> It is finished

IT IS THE MERCY…
It is the end of my
my game the TRUTH
has been revealed and it will
be done as my family require me
to do it.

On 10 July the Royal Mail ship *Picardy* spotted a small trimaran drifting under slack sails with no one in the cockpit. On
boarding it they saw the yacht to be in bad shape, with fittings
and equipment missing. The empty cabin was a squalid den,
dirty dishes filled the sink. Bits of radio equipment lay scattered everywhere and coloured wires peeled loosely from the
walls, leading into the computer locker. When its waterproof
seal was removed, the space was found to contain only a
tangled mass of wiring. The computer had only ever existed in
Crowhurst's head.

❧

In the Antarctic Richard Byrd had been alone at the weather
station since 28 March. It was now late July. He was ill and weak,
his notes on the period are sparse, and the account he wrote later
in *Alone* is not the full record. If, like Crowhurst, he strayed
into the dark forest during the long night, he destroyed those
pages. We have no direct access to his true state of mind; we
can reconstruct it only from his later behaviour – which we will
come to in the next chapter.

At Little America there had been growing concern about his
condition since April when the pattern of his morse messages
had become confused and at time indecipherable. Dr Poulter
and Charles Murphy suspected he was ill and concealing the
fact; they decided he must be rescued. On 4 August Poulter

set out with two men in the most reliable of the snow tractors, driving along the uncertain trail by headlights, for it was still night. On 10 August they reached Bolling Advance Weather Base and retrieved Byrd, abandoning the weather station. He was gaunt, emaciated, and not a well man. While he recovered physically at Little America during the months which followed, many flights were made to the interior of the continent, proving that it was not divided into two but a single landmass. Also – as promised – discovering new lands, and asserting a territorial claim in the name of the United States to most of the Pacific quadrant of Antarctica, a landmass amounting to hundreds of thousands of square miles, together with all the mineral wealth that it contained.

Having thus achieved its aims, in the spring of 1935 the expedition and its leader returned to America where Admiral Byrd received the welcome commensurate to his success. It was a great time to come home. Prohibition was repealed, Franklin Roosevelt had been elected President to the music of his campaign song, *Happy Days Are Here Again*, the New Deal was beginning to deliver and America had started on the slow climb back toward prosperity. Byrd spoke about his triumph in 156 cities to an audience of 600,000 people, and on the radio to millions, to all America. His place in history was assured. His public persona of the explorer hero had become a national brand, extending to today.

31.

FINAL ACT

The scene is the North Pole. Summer 1947.

Wisps of flimsy cirrus cloud slowly drift away south, the haze dissolves and the sun is revealed floating in a pale Arctic sky like an enormous fuzzy peach diffusing a glaze of radiance across the frozen ocean below, as Bernt Balchen banks the aeroplane he is piloting into a steep turn to complete a full circuit of the North Pole in less than a couple of minutes. In a four-engine C54, to fly over this spot is now a routine achievement effected regularly by the large aircraft of the day, which bear little resemblance to the primitive machines that struggled towards this same goal in the race to reach The Pole first, more than two decades ago. Yet the manner in which this particular flight will end is *not* routine, for it triggers events which in no way can be foreseen by Balchen when he throws the stick hard over to execute that wilful turn around the potent yet invisible icon on the ice below, in the course of a flight from Fairbanks, Alaska to Thule in Greenland. It will incite the first of a series of increasingly menacing confrontations with Admiral Richard Byrd, whom he has not seen for fourteen years...

Balchen's career has flourished in the long interval. In 1935 he was appointed deputy manager of the newly formed Norwegian national airline. A year later he went to Washington to look for a US airline to partner it in a regular transatlantic route. A chance encounter with Postmaster General James Farley led to a meeting with President Roosevelt and a deal with Pan American Airways. In 1938 Balchen visited Berlin to order aeroplane parts from the Junkers factory, and observed production lines staffed by 20,000 workers turning out Stuka bombers. While standing on the balcony of his room at the Kaiserhof Hotel he watched Adolf Hitler stir up a rapturous congregation of a quarter-million crowded into the square below, and glimpsed the future. In 1940 Balchen, with his family, was back in New York as Norway's military representative in the US, and in 1941 he was given the rank of captain, assisting Major-General Arnold, head of the Air Corps, and engaged with him in the awesome task of transforming the nation's less than one thousand planes into the most mighty air force in the world. America was about to go to war. By 1943 he was attached to the OSS, flying missions to drop arms to underground resistance groups in Nazi-occupied Norway. He was a veteran of Arctic adventure who had not lost a taste for its excitements. Up to the end of the conflict in 1945 Balchen enjoyed what was known at the time as 'a good war'.

After completing a lap around the North Pole, Balchen set a course for Thule, the American airbase now established in the north of Greenland. Having taken off from Fairbanks, Alaska, his flight route there was far from a direct one. The Pole was a whimsical diversion, however the way he relates his arrival in Thule that day strikes the reader as disingenuous:

> We landed on a gravel strip at the base of the mountains ...
> As I was filling out my Form I a sergeant of the crew scratched

his head. 'Look Colonel, weren't you pilot on the South Pole flight too?'

I nodded absently as I was writing. '*Ja*, sure. Why?'

'Well then, don't that make you the first man who ever piloted a plane over both Poles?'

'I guess it does,' I said. It hadn't occurred to me until that moment.

Balchen's account is engagingly self-deprecatory, but is hardly rendered credible by the fact that he flew on to attend a press conference scheduled in Washington. To fly to the North Pole was no longer an event of note, but to have piloted a plane to *both* rated at least a paragraph and photo in the newspaper. However, on arrival at the Pentagon he found the press conference cancelled and a message to report to the office of Admiral Richard Byrd.

Byrd did not get up from behind his desk when he came in, neither did he offer him a seat. Balchen was greatly struck by his appearance, he'd aged considerably since he'd last seen him. He'd lost flesh and shrunk within his uniform and that buoyant vitality once so electric to encounter was no longer present in his manner. His hair had thinned and his face soured, he'd become an old man with an old man's agitated and testy bearing. Balchen's wife, Bess, jotted down the words of this conversation when her husband described the meeting later that evening:

Byrd asked about the flight and my work in Alaska, then about my flying status. I showed him my green instrument card. He then asked who had given me permission to make the flight. Byrd then looked at me in anger and said, 'If you think that you will get a promotion to general in the Air Force, just forget it. Not over my dead body, I'll see to that!'

Balchen was startled and upset by the encounter. He had done nothing to damage Byrd's reputation: very much the contrary, he'd always spoken highly of his remarkable ability. Bess and he discussed the matter that night, coming to the conclusion that Byrd not only resented Balchen for piloting a plane to both Poles, but feared he might reveal what he knew about Byrd's North Pole 'win'. For certainly he realised that, on Balchen's extensive tour around the US in the *Jo Ford* which followed that 'win', Balchen must have figured out that the Pole flight was not possible in the time. He knew Balchen knew and was an enemy who could betray him. The demon of retribution lurking in the shadows of Byrd's mind had taken human shape and wore Balchen's face.

Paranoia is a medical condition most succinctly described as a growing anxiety directed toward the future. It is usually founded on something real, people rarely become paranoid for no good reason. It can occur gradually or without warning, brought on by shock or poisoning. Carbon monoxide is known sometimes to induce psychotic symptoms. Paranoia involves guilt, shame, apprehension, suspicion, sense of persecution, jealousy and anger. With it comes an over-reaction to trivia and misinterpretation of commonplace events. The individual believes these random events relate directly to *them*, and that everything *means* some-thing. Often this is accompanied by auditory hallucinations. The paranoid person hears various voices commenting on his/her behaviour, arguing between themselves, echoing their thoughts derisively, or instructing them to commit particular actions. Many things seem to confirm these delusions, the sufferer becomes unable to discriminate between fantasy and reality. Psychiatrists claim that deep within their subconscious the guilty individual believes he deserves to be exposed and punished.

Following that confrontation over Balchen's polar circuit, he and Admiral Byrd did not meet again for another three years. By then Balchen had been posted to Washington. There he was assigned a closet-sized office in the basement of the Pentagon, without a telephone or even a chair for visitors – not that he received many, for he was given no work. Frustrated, he passed his time in the Pentagon library, occasionally travelling to some city to attend a function and deliver a speech for the Air Force.

In the spring of 1952 the Balchens attended a funeral service for Dana Coman, who had been on Byrd's second Antarctic expedition. At the reception afterwards Balchen spotted the Admiral among a group of people. Approaching him, Balchen attempted to introduce his wife. 'Byrd looked at us with a glare cold as all of the Polar Regions. Then he quickly turned away, chatting with everyone else,' reports Bess Balchen. A month later Balchen was at home one weekend when he was surprised to receive a call from Byrd, who made no reference to their non-encounter but instead was oddly affable. He said he wanted to meet to discuss arrangements for the twenty-fifth anniversary of their transatlantic flight, would Balchen be in town next week? Balchen confirmed he would and Byrd said he'd be in touch to fix a date. 'When are they going to make you a general?' Byrd asked. 'It won't be long now, I know.' Byrd never followed up on his call, no meeting took place.

In January 1953 *Reader's Digest* ran a piece titled 'Bernt Balchen, Viking of the Air'. The magazine's editor received a letter from Admiral Byrd, objecting to the article's misplaced emphasis on Balchen. On 5 October *Newsweek* published another piece about him: 'Will the Air Force fire a great Arctic expert? Deep in the basement of the Pentagon ... sits a man with one of the great names in American aviation. Neglect and rigid military regulations may soon force him to retire in his early fifties...' A week afterward Balchen ran into the Admiral at a ceremony at Kitty Hawk commemorating the fiftieth anniversary of the Wright Brothers' flight. Bess Balchen says that when her husband came home that night he was white with anger. Byrd had threatened him. At her insistence he sat down to document their conversation.

> As we were going out of the hall he (REB) pulled out a clipping of the article in *Newsweek* … He said, 'I am going to let you know right away that the publicity you … are getting has got to stop. If you do not take care of this immediately I am going to see to it that this is done. Many of my influential friends are tired of the way you are taking credit for a lot of things you never did and are getting recognition which you do not deserve, you can include me in this too. Do not ever believe for a moment that I will stand for being stepped on by you.' Byrd then reminded me he was the one who brought me over to the States … he could have stopped my regular commission at any time by just lifting his finger. Here he became furious and said, 'I held it long enough.'

Balchen was so angry he reported the encounter to the Air Force Public Relations Office, who called him in to question him on his account. Later, after discussing what he should do with Bess, Balchen wrote Byrd a letter:

> Dear Dick, This is to tell you that, as requested by you, I have related our conversation at Kitty Hawk to the USAF public relations office … I believe that after you have given more thought to this matter you will realise that I have never said or done anything that could have been detrimental to you. Quite the opposite. Sincerely, Bernt.

A week later the Balchens were in the SAS departure lounge at Idlewild (now Kennedy) Airport, about to take off on a short trip to Norway, when Bernt was told there was a call for him from Boston. Balchen had to take it in the Despatch Office, surrounded by activity and noise. Byrd demanded to know why Balchen was flying to Norway. What was his business there? Why had he repeated their Kitty Hawk conversation to the Air Force? He ordered Balchen to stop making false claims and trying to discredit him. Amid the hubbub of the Despatch Office Bess was attempting frantically to take notes of what was said. Often Byrd told Balchen to speak louder. Balchen was left with the strong impression he was taping their conversation.

The Balchens were back in the US on 1 November when Drew Pearson on the *Washington Post* ran a garbled account of the incident at Kitty Hawk:

> … two Arctic explorers who almost got into a fist fight … Byrd backed Balchen into a corner and shouted angry threats at him … flew into a rage, accused the bewildered Balchen of stealing the limelight, and threatened to use political connections to wreck his Air Force career … Balchen flushed an angry red, but friends interceded before things got out of hand.

The item provoked Byrd to call Balchen's home number several times in the middle of the night. When Bess told him her husband was not there he slammed the phone down. On 8 November Byrd telephoned during the evening. Having got Balchen on the line he told him to hold on while he changed telephones. Their conversation was stilted, for Byrd seemed to be under strain. Again Balchen felt certain it was taped. Afterwards he sent the Admiral a short letter: 'Dear Dick, I am glad you called, and believe that I have interpreted your remarks correctly. I must tell you quite truthfully that I was shocked and surprised at the accusations you made. However I hope these most unpleasant occurrences are now over…'

They were not. On 13 November Byrd replied: 'Dear Balchen, Neither of your letters was called for.' He says that he now realises that he's up against an enemy of 'utter ruthlessness' who will 'utilise any method to attain the end desired'. He suspects that someone else is helping Balchen who must be a 'bitter enemy of mine' to be part of such malevolence and warns him that if he and co-conspirators think 'that I've become a weakling with no ability to defend myself' they are very much mistaken. He reminds him that he has powerful friends.

To Bernt and Bess Balchen the words seemed the raving of a man in the grip of runaway paranoia. Balchen replied in the last note he would write to Byrd: 'Dear Dick, Your letter has me completely nonplussed. I do not know what you are driving at. All I can say in answering it is to repeat and stress what I have said before, that I have never said or done anything that could have been detrimental to you. I have always expressed my gratitude for what you have done for me in the past.' It was so. And it was also true that in the past Byrd had been reciprocally grateful to Balchen. He had publicly credited him as a superb pilot, a brilliant mechanic, and testified to his many-sided abilities. He'd said Balchen was capable, trustworthy and, even more important on an extended polar expedition, 'he always played the game'. Balchen had, and look where playing the game had got him. He was a man of even temper, not prone to rancour; he had a slow fuse but it was well lit by now and smouldering. He remained in his basement cubicle in the Pentagon without a telephone, without work, and without promotion. In February he received a formal dressing down from his superior officer who, demanded what right he had to travel to Philadelphia to speak at an Army Ordinance dinner.

Despite the inconvenience of no chair to seat him in, Balchen did receive a visitor in April 1954. This was Byrd's close friend Dr James Mooney, who came with a suggestion as to how the unfortunate misunderstanding with the Admiral might be settled amicably on both sides. He proposed that a magazine article should be written about Byrd, the distinguished 66-year-old national hero who had so inspired his epoch with the idea of flight. It would pay due tribute to his skills as an aviator and navigator, as an explorer and charismatic leader. Mooney suggested that Balchen should byline this article with his own name and receive the fee for authorship. If he agreed to do so he had the guarantee of Senator Harry Byrd (Byrd's brother) and the Admiral himself that he would be promoted brigadier-general within ninety days.

Balchen was still only a colonel when he retired from the Air Force two years later. His first significant act as a civilian was to sign a contract with the New York publisher E. P. Dutton to write his autobiography. He'd taken enough shit. He had a story to tell.

It was a bold move. Both Balchen and Bess felt an understandable nervousness. In choosing to confront Byrd they were taking on the Navy and the establishment, represented by his family and influential connections. But having made that move, the couple decided to make another equally significant. Flying to Norway, they met with Professor Sverdrug, a meteorologist and Arctic expert, and Gosta Liljequist, professor of meteorology at Uppsala University. Liljequist (who was planning to spend that winter in Spitsbergen) agreed to collate all weather data from around the Arctic rim for the period of Byrd's flight, and to analyse and prepare a report.*

---

* It would be wearisome for the reader to wade through the dossier here, but this is available together with a detailed account of the Balchen/Byrd conflict, published by Bess Balchen on http://home.acadia.net/userpages/kikut/BBMainText.htm. Anyone further interested can examine the subject in the exhaustive archive at Ohio State University, where the collection of papers documenting the life and career of Admiral Richard E. Byrd

To transform Balchen's material into a publishable memoir the Balchens struck a deal with the journalist Corey Ford. Having embarked on the book, Bess was every whit as determined as her husband in going through with it, come what may. She'd been at Balchen's side through lean times and good ever since he'd returned to America from the South Pole flight with Byrd. She knew he'd sought none of that glory and profit for himself – nor had he been offered it. He'd been denied a medal, denied promotion, now even due recognition was being denied him. It was grossly unjust, and her grip upon the sword of retribution was resolute as his own.

Nevertheless both of them experienced moments of anxiety. By challenging Byrd they were challenging a myth. They discussed the book with Francis Drake, a journalist friend, and with Dr Larry Gould, the amiable scientist who had been second-in-command on Byrd's first Antarctic expedition. 'It might backfire, we know his power,' Drake cautioned them. Gould said he fully realised Byrd had not made it to the North Pole 'but they could crucify you'.

In March 1957 Admiral Byrd died in Boston. His funeral, attended by everyone of note, was a grand and solemn occasion appropriate to a national hero holding the Congressional Medal of Honor. The Vice-President was there together with a fraternity of the great and good to honour him as a role model to American youth.

In February 1958 the pages of Balchen's book were already printed, but the edition had not yet been bound. 'Then', says Bess Balchen, 'All hell broke loose.' Richard E. Byrd Jnr, went to see Elliot Macrae, president of E.P. Dutton. Washington, the Navy, the family and an army of lawyers descended upon Dutton

---

amounts to 523 cubic feet. But before visiting either of these sites, perhaps read this book to the end.

in well-funded massed attack. Under such pressure the book was radically amended. Any criticism of Byrd and all questions about his flight to the North Pole were excised from the manuscript. The book was issued without promotion in a limited print run, received no attention, failed to recover its advance and was remaindered.

32.

CURTAIN CALL

Did Byrd reach the North Pole?

Professor Liljequist's meteorological findings conclude that the following winds Byrd claimed to have assisted his flight did not exist. The speeds he asserted were without substance, therefore his flight to the Pole and back was impossible in the time. There are further inconsistencies to his 'win'. On his historic journey Byrd did not keep a flight log, as is customary. The evidence for his success, which he submitted to the National Geographic Society, consisted only of his diary and a notebook. These controversial documents were published by Ohio State University in 1998. The diary includes messages he passed to his pilot, Floyd Bennett. One instructs him, 'Radio that we have reached the Pole and are returning with one motor with bad oil leak but expect to make Spitsbergen'. But it also contains still legible erasures of navigational calculations and the note to Bennett, 'How long were we gone before we turned around?' If he had got to the Pole surely he would have known *that*, for the time must have formed the basis to his calculation that they had reached it.

Perhaps he was concerned with different arithmetic. If he failed in this endeavour his newspaper, publishing and product endorsement contracts were worthless, he could not hope to pay back his debts, he was ruined. The family home in Boston would have to go, his children be removed from private school, his career end in shameful bankruptcy. The bottom line to his calculations, financial and navigational, was that he literally couldn't afford *not* to reach the Pole.

It is for the reader to judge Byrd's achievement. He was a man of probity and honour. To conceive a fraud was foreign (perhaps fatal) to his nature. And, one wonders, *how* exactly was that fraud concocted between himself and Bennett in a cabin so noisy verbal exchange was impossible and all communication had to be by means of scribbled notes? How do you agree the detail of a lifetime's deception in a few pencilled words blocked out on a scrap of paper in an ice-cold vibrating plane? A contract to duplicity which, once concluded, is shredded and scattered on the Arctic wind, never to be referred to again.

And there is another possibility. Perhaps such a contract was never discussed. When, after the oil leak, Byrd ordered Bennett to circle while they saw how it developed, Bennett knew full well the attempt on the Pole was over. The fact must have been crushing, particularly for Byrd. Perhaps they passed no notes but remained silent, numbed by defeat or in denial. Not until their plane landed and that crowd of ecstatic fans came racing down the slope to greet them... not until then was Byrd driven to respond, and came up with the reaction psychologically forced upon him by their expectation. Given the consequences, it makes for a curious perception but, as Byrd observed himself, life turns upon a dime.

The most compelling human testimony to Byrd's deception exists in a letter Bernt Balchen wrote to an enquirer in 1960:

For many years I thought Byrd himself would tell the truth about his flight ... but after the war, while I was in Washington, Byrd tried everything to make my life miserable, I … started to collect data, fully intent on giving out the story as soon as I was out of uniform. Byrd must have known all along that I knew the truth, and this must have been the reason for his behaviour. My big disappointment was that he passed away before I was able to get it out … I had simply stated what I know to be a fact, that he had not reached the North Pole on his flight in 1926. I know this for two reasons, first, because the plane was incapable of making this flight in 15½ hours … *and secondly because Floyd Bennett told me so.*

So it would seem Byrd lied… and as a result of that one historic lie he found the glory, the success, celebrity, respect and gratifying elevation to the ranks of the great and good which accompanies fame. For more than thirty years and until his death he lived the life of a public figure, attending banquets, delivering speeches, an honoured guest wherever he went. But the pedestal he stood upon was made of clay; all the time he knew he was a fraud – and so did another man. Inevitably the result was paranoia. What terrors must have swarmed around his mind as he lay sleepless in the long watches of the night with no one to confess to, no hope of absolution.

The imagination falters in assessing the price Byrd paid for his fraud; the cost to others can be more precisely determined. Among the contenders who set their hearts on flying first to the North Pole only Ellsworth escaped unscathed. His marriage proved happy, his fortune grew; his ambition to be an explorer was never wholly fulfilled but he stayed true to the frontier tradition which inspired him. His name is unsung today, but he remains an understated American hero.

Umberto Nobile – stripped of his rank, disgraced and ostracised after the disaster of the *Italia* expedition – emigrated to Russia, where he built airships for the government. There, his emotional nature led him to embrace Communism as a solution to this unfair world. He did so, as we might expect, *con brio*, putting fame and notoriety behind him. After Mussolini's death in 1945, he returned to Italy (with his family though no longer Tintina), was rehabilitated, and elected a Communist deputy in 1948. The author's father, who knew him in Milan, describes him as a benign, loquacious old man who passed his days on a café terrace, telling stories to strangers happy to pay for his drinks – which is not necessarily a sad end for those it suits.

And Balchen, whose courage and achievement were equal to the rest, what did he receive in return? Not recognition, not a medal, not promotion with a general's pension. Yet there were rewards: a new life as an American, a happy marriage, a son and wife so true her widowhood was devoted to the vindication of his name. More than most men's, Balchen's life was fully lived.

So now the tale is told, the show is over. At the end of this epic drama the members of the cast now step forward individually to take their curtain call. They have played their parts and await our judgement, derision or applause. Only Amundsen yet remains to be acknowledged, that old man who towers like an ancient oak among these other trees. It is he who has suffered the hardest cut from Byrd's deception. Condemned by it to remain bankrupt, suspect and diminished, not only was he denied the prize which would have restored his fortune and reputation, but the sequel cost him his life. Condemned to ignominious retirement, he'd put aside his rusty sword... then received a final trumpet call to arms. He'd been summoned by his country once again, called forth one last time to plight his troth. He'd flown north to rescue Nobile, a fool he despised. And in that gesture, that final gracious act of a proud and upright man, he went down forever on the great white silence of the ice. A little stiffly he takes his bow, the last to leave the stage.

Byrd – Lied   Amundsen – Died   Nobile – Exiled

Ellsworth – Disowned   Balchen – Betrayed

ACKNOWLEDGEMENTS

'd like to thank several people who have contributed to this book in one way or another: Stephen Brough; Peter Mayle; Peter Nichols, Ernest Chapman; my agent Julian Friedmann. At Biteback my editor Sam Carter, James Stephens, Katy Scholes and Emma Young. My thanks also to the picture editor Nina Risoli, to Gill Hoffs for research and to Christine Groom at Valiant Services.

BIBLIOGRAPHY

This is not a work of history. It is a narrative account of a race, together with an examination of its principal contestants. My main sources are the reports which they and others wrote about the experience and their subsequent lives. I am most grateful to their inheritors.

Amundsen, Roald, *My Life as an Explorer* (William Heinemann, 1927)

Amundsen & Ellsworth, *The First Flight across the Polar Sea* (Hutchinson & Co., 1927)

Balchen, Bernt, *Come North with Me* (E. P. Dutton & Co., 1958)

Byrd, Richard, *Alone* (G. P. Putnam's Sons, 1938)

Byrd, Richard, *Exploring with Byrd* (G. P. Putnam's Sons, 1937)

Ellsworth, Lincoln, *Beyond Horizons* (William Heinemann, 1938)

Freuchen, Peter, *Book of the Eskimos* (The World Publishing Co., 1961)

Hoyt, Edwin P., *The Last Explorer* (The John Day Company, 1968)

Jenkins, Alan, *The Twenties* (Heinemann, 1974)

Jenkins, Alan, *The Thirties* (Heinemann, 1976)

à Kempis, Thomas, *The Imitation of Christ* (Roswoyd, Atwerp, 1617)

Leighton, Isabel, *The Aspirin Age 1919–1941* (Simon and Schuster, 1949)

Merton, Thomas, *No Man is an Island* (Burns and Oates, 1955)

Nichols, Peter, *A Voyage for Madmen* (HarperCollins, 2001)

Nobile, Umberto, *My Polar Flights* (Frederick Muller, 1961)

Owen, Russell, *South of the Sun* (The John Day Company, 1934)

Pool, Beekman H., *Polar Extremes* (University of Alaska Press, 2002)

Scott, J. M., *The Private Life of Polar Exploration* (William Blackwood, 1982)

Underhill, Evelyn, *Mysticism: A Study in the Nature and Development of Man's Spiritual Consciousness* (Metheun, 1911)

INDEX